I wish I could come home. I think I'll die if I have to be like this much longer. Won't someone tell me why all this had to happen to me? Daddy please do what the man tells you or he'll kill me if you don't.

PS. Please Daddy. I want to come home tonight.

BOOKS IN THE DEAD MEN DO TELL TALES SERIES

Dead Men Do Tell Tales (2008)

Bloody Chicago (2006)

Bloody Illinois (2008)

Bloody Hollywood (2008)

Without a Trace (2009)

Blood, Guns & Valentines (2010)

Murdered in Their Beds (2012)

Fallen Angel (2013)

Murder by Gaslight (2013)

Fear the Reaper (with Rene Kruse) (2014)

One August Morning (2015)

The Two Lost Girls (2015)

One Night at the Biograph (2016)

I Want to Come Home Tonight (2017)

The Dead Men Do Tell Tales Series

"I WANT TO COME HOME TONIGHT"

The Haunting Story of Marion Parker

TROY TAYLOR

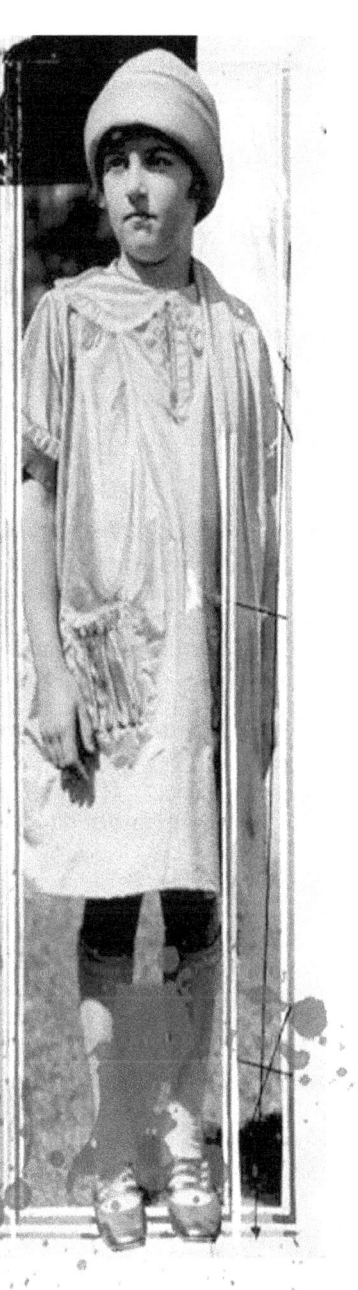

© Copyright 2017 by Troy Taylor & American Hauntings Ink
All Rights Reserved, including the right to copy or reproduce this book, or portions thereof, in any form, without express permission from the author and publisher.

Original Cover Artwork Designed by
© Copyright 2017 by April Slaughter & Troy Taylor

This Book is Published By:
American Hauntings Ink
Jacksonville, Illinois | 217.791.7859
Visit us on the Internet at http://www.americanhauntingsink.com

First Edition – June 2017
ISBN: 978-1-892523-83-9

Printed in the United States of America

DECEMBER 17, 1927

Perry Parker nervously drove his automobile down the shadowy street. His hands were gripped tightly on the steering wheel and he anxiously glanced into the rearview mirror, praying silently that the police were not following him this time. On the previous night, the kidnapper had called with ransom instructions, but he had been spooked when he saw police vehicles trailing Parker's car.

The next morning, Parker received another special delivery letter –- another hastily scrawled message from the man who had kidnapped his beloved daughter, Marion. Once again, the kidnapper had demanded money for Marion's return –- a bizarrely small amount of money to ask for, especially from a man of Parker's apparent wealth. The kidnapped girl's father was an officer at the Los Angeles First National Trust and Savings Bank and yet the kidnapper had only asked for a paltry $1,500.

The letter was much like the others he had received since his daughter had vanished. The kidnapper admonished him for involving the police and laid out what he called his "final chance terms" for getting Marion back alive. A second letter was enclosed in the envelope from the kidnapper. The second note was a handwritten plea from his daughter, ending with the heart-wrenching words, "Please Daddy. I want to come home tonight."

Parker was determined to let nothing stand in the way of his daughter being returned. Slipping away from vigilant detectives, he drove away in his Essex automobile with a wrapped bundle of cash on the seat next to him. It was nearly 8:00 p.m. when he arrived near Fifth Street and Manhattan Place, where the kidnapper told him they would meet. He was to remain in his car, hand over the money and wait as the kidnapper drove a short distance up the street and let Marion out on the side of the road.

The meeting place was six miles north of the original rendezvous point, which meant a longer drive for Parker. It also gave the kidnapper more time to follow him and to check and see if he was being followed by the police. While he was driving, Parker constantly checked his rearview mirror, trying to see if there were cars behind him. He had been stern with the police, insisting that they should not follow him. They agreed, and yet he could not be sure.

Nothing in Perry Parker's life as a successful businessman could have prepared him for the nightmare he now faced. He had spent the last two days in the grip of unrelenting fear with his wife, Geraldine. She had paced the floors of her room, barely conscious of who or where she was. The chilling letters had demanded cash and threatened horror. There were telephone calls and more threats. The Parkers had faced two days of hell on earth and, if asked, Parker would have said that nothing could surprise him now.

He was wrong.

Parker stopped his car at Manhattan Place, and switched off the engine. A few minutes later, a Chrysler roadster pulled up alongside of him. He could see the kidnapper in the shadows, a white handkerchief pulled up over the lower half of his face. In the dim light, Parker could see his daughter on the seat next to the man. She was covered with a blanket. As the roadster eased to a stop, the kidnapper level a gun on the edge of the window. The muzzle was pointed at Parker's face. He demanded the money and in return, Parker asked to see his daughter. The kidnapper pulled back the edge of the blanket and her father could see the little girl. She was wide-eyed and silent, likely terrified by her ordeal. She was there for only a moment and then slipped back out of sight.

"All right, now the money," the man said to him.

As Parker leaned out his window to pass it between the two cars, the kidnapper reached over Marion to receive it. Their hands were mere inches apart as he grasped the bundle of bills -- $1,500 in new $20 gold certificate bills, the serial numbers of which had been carefully recorded by the authorities -- and the shotgun wavered less than two feet from Parker's face. He felt a cold trickle of sweat go down his back.

Parker swallowed his fear and focused on his daughter. "Are you going to give her to me?" he asked.

The stranger spoke to him in a soft voice. "Don't follow me, and be careful. I'll drive up there and put her out, and you can get her."

The roadster moved slowly down the street and paused in the gloom in front of 432 Manhattan Place. Parker tried to see the license number, but both ends of the plate were bent over, hiding the first and last digits. Giving up, he concentrated on the driver, waiting for him to get out of the car. Instead, the passenger door swung open for a moment, then slammed shut again. The roadster roared off at full speed and vanished into the darkness. Marion had been dumped out on the lawn like a bundle of garbage.

As soon as the kidnapper's tail lights disappeared, Parker threw open his door and rushed frantically to his daughter's side. Marion had been wrapped in a blanket, which her father pulled away from her. She tumbled out onto the sidewalk. He knelt on the hard pavement, calling out Marion's name, but she did not respond.

Parker peered closer -- there was something wrong with her eyes. The child's face had been powdered, her hair combed and brushed. Her eyelids were tied open with bits of black thread. Parker -- despite the promise that he had made to himself to control his emotions -- wailed in agony. He swept his daughter up into his arms and realized that the figure was too small to be Marion. He eased her limp body back to the pavement. Tears stung his eyes as he fumbled with the blanket, pulling aside one corner and then another. For one frozen moment, he could only stare in shock -- and then he began to scream.

His daughter felt small because her arms and legs were missing.

With a loud, anguished cry, Perry Parker pulled the remains of his murdered and mutilated daughter to his chest and began to weep in agony. Every parents' worst nightmare had just been realized by an unassuming bank officer who had no idea why his family had been chosen to be visited by such horror.

THE "SNATCH RACKET"

In the summer of 1874, a four-year-old boy named Charlie Ross was kidnapped near his parent's home in Germantown, Pennsylvania. The men who took him demanded a ransom of $20,000 -- well over half a million dollars today -- and promised to kill the boy if his parents refused to pay.

The boy's father, Christian Ross, was advised by the police to stall for time. He could promise the ransom, but take his time in paying it, allowing the police to search for the boy. Ross took out newspaper ads, claiming that he was arranging for the money, while the police scoured the city and countryside. They had no experience with such a crime -- no one did in those days -- and were used to dealing with horse theft and murder, not stolen children.

Charlie Ross

The kidnappers replied to the newspaper ads, writing more than two dozen letters that were each more threatening than the last. Finally, Ross agreed to meet the kidnappers but they never arrived at the rendezvous.

Charlie was never seen again.

Not the real Charlie Ross anyway. Sightings of the "lost boy" occurred all over the country. As time went on -- months, then years -- scores of teenage boys claimed to be Charlie. None of them were. Even P.T. Barnum -- well-aware of the kidnapping's publicity value -- got into the act. He offered a $10,000 personal reward for the boy's return. He got the publicity that he was looking for, but not Charlie.

Charlie's name was kept alive well into the 1880s. Songs were written, trinkets sold, and his father penned a best-selling book about the missing lad. Each year, the anniversary of the kidnapping was marked by the press and the story retold.

As late as 1939, the story was still making news. A 69-year-old man in Phoenix, Arizona, filed papers in court in an attempt to establish his identity as the missing boy. His efforts failed.

Historians have named the Ross case as the first kidnapping for ransom in American history, and perhaps it was. However, because kidnapping was rare, only a handful of jurisdictions acknowledged it as a specific crime in those days. Yet, kidnapping, for a variety of purposes, is as old as recorded history.

It was the press that made the Ross case so important. For whatever reason, it captured the attention of reporters, who fed it to a nation that was hungry for sensation news. Newspapers across the land devoted untold column inches to the story, and they continued to do so long after it stopped being news. Publishers, editors, and circulation managers discovered that sensational crime stories -- especially those that put children into peril -- sold more newspapers.

But cases like that of Charlie Ross remained isolated crimes until the second decade of the twentieth century. Still, the ability of kidnapping to stir hearts, minds, and pocketbooks did not go unnoticed. During the early days of film, kidnapping was a popular subject. Villains who ran off with beautiful maidens -- often tying them to the railroad tracks to be rescued by the hero -- was a mainstay of silent films. Lurid depictions of kidnappings were so popular in Chicago's nickelodeons that police were compelled to confiscate films and outlaw the genre. They feared that the picture shows might incite the genuine crime.

Exploitation aside, kidnapping was a serious and deadly business. For reasons long debated by historians, ransom kidnapping entered its heyday at the end of World War I, as America was entering the Jazz Age of the 1920s. It thrived over the next two decades.

Certainly, Prohibition -- and the explosion of organized crime that came about because of it -- played a significant role in the emergence of kidnapping as a means of influencing events and, theoretically at least, quickly acquiring a big pile of money.

During this era, competition among various gangs was intense and ruthless. Bootlegging was a huge business and gun-point abductions became a means to achieving various ends. It was an efficient method of intimidation, persuasion, and elimination. A very large number of so-called "one-way rides" ended up with a rival gangster shot to death in a ditch or wearing concrete overshoes at the bottom of a river. Ransom kidnappings occurred, as well, and large sums of money and liquor territories were frequently exchanged between gangs.

Kidnapping became a cottage industry and its frequency sent reporters scurrying for descriptive phrases for the crime. By the early 1920s, the "snatch racket" was coined and the name stuck.

Not surprisingly, the gangster kidnappings made headlines and provoked copycat crimes. For instance, in 1926, famed Los Angeles evangelist Aimee Semple McPherson disappeared from Venice Beach. Presumed drowned, she was miraculously resurrected a few weeks later in Douglas, Arizona, with a melodramatic tale of kidnapping and torture in Mexico. The story fell apart and it was learned that her disappearance actually took her -- and her lover -- to a cabin by the sea at Carmel.

But real abductions that were carried out by amateurs were risky propositions -- for perpetrators and victims alike. Money-hungry improvisors didn't have the patience or the skills of the professionals and, all too often, panicked reactions to unanticipated events led to the death of the captive.

And the deaths weren't always by accident because some kidnappings had nothing to do with greed.

THE "PERFECT CRIME"

On May 21, 1924, the sons of two of Chicago's wealthiest and most illustrious families drove to the Harvard School on the city's South Side and kidnapped a young boy named Bobby Franks. Their plan was to carry out the "perfect murder." It was a scheme so devious that only two men of superior intellect -- such as their own, they believed -- could accomplish it. The two young men, Richard Loeb and Nathan Leopold, were the privileged heirs of prominent families who decided to kidnap and kill a child for the pure thrill of it. They considered themselves "brilliant" -- a belief that led to their downfall.

Nathan Leopold, or "Babe" as his friends knew him, was born in 1906 and from an early age, had a number of sexual encounters, starting with the advances of a governess and culminating in a relationship with Richard Loeb. He excelled at school and was 18 when he graduated from the University of Chicago. He was an expert ornithologist and botanist and spoke nine languages fluently. His mother died when he was young and his father had little interest in him. He compensated for this with lavish amounts of money, expensive vacations, an automobile, and hefty weekly allowance.

Richard Loeb was the son of the Vice President of Sears & Roebuck and while he came from a family as wealthy as Leopold's, he was merely a clever young man and far from brilliant. He was, however, quite handsome and charming and what he lacked in intelligence, he more than made up for in arrogance. Both of them were obsessed with perfection. To them, perfection meant being above all others, which their station in life endorsed. They felt they were immune to laws and criticism, which meant they were perfect.

Richard Loeb and Nathan Leopold: Chicago's infamous "Thrill Killers"

Bored, Loeb fantasized about committing the "perfect crime." With his more docile companion in tow, he began developing what he believed to be a foolproof scheme. Leopold, easily dominated by his friend, agreed to join him in a series of always escalating crimes. They began with robbery and petty theft and worked their way up to arson and vandalism, but this was not enough for Loeb. He dreamed of something bigger. A murder, he convinced his friend, would be their greatest intellectual challenge.

They developed a plan over the next seven months. They would kidnap someone and make it appear as though the person was being held for ransom. They would send ransom notes, promising the victim's safe return, but that would never happen. They were going to murder their captive.

One afternoon in May, they rented a car and drove to a hardware store at 43rd and Cottage Avenue in Chicago, where they bought some rope, a chisel, and a bottle of hydrochloric acid. The plan was to strangle their victim, stab him with the chisel if necessary, and then destroy his identity with the acid.

On the morning after their hardware store trip, they met at Leopold's home and wrapped the handle of the chisel with adhesive tape so that it offered a better grip. They also found a blanket and tore some strips of cloth that could be used to wrap up and bind their victim. Leopold placed a pair of wading boots in the car because the boys planned to deposit the body in the swamps near Wolf Lake, located south of the city. They packed loaded pistols for each of them and looked over a ransom note that had been written on a typewriter that had been stolen from Loeb's old fraternity house at the University of Michigan. The note demanded $10,000 in cash. Neither of them needed the money but they felt the note would convince the authorities that the kidnappers were lowly, money-hungry criminals and deflect attention from people like Leopold and Loeb.

They had only overlooked one thing -- a victim.

They first considered killing Loeb's younger brother, Tommy, but they discarded that idea. It was not because Tommy was a family member but only because it would have been hard for Loeb to collect the ransom money without arousing suspicion. They also considering killing Armand Deutsch, grandson of millionaire philanthropist Julius Rosenwald, but also dismissed this idea because Rosenwald was the president of Sears & Roebuck and Loeb's father's immediate boss. They also came close to agreeing to kill their friend, Richard Rubel, who regularly had lunch with them. Rubel was ruled out, not because he was a good friend to them, but because they knew his father was cheap and would never agree to pay the ransom.

They could not agree on anyone but did feel that their victim should be small, so that he could be easily subdued. With that in mind, they decided to check out the Harvard Preparatory School, which was located across the street from Leopold's home. They climbed into their rental car and began to drive. As they drove, Leopold noticed some boys near Ellis Avenue and Loeb pointed out one of them that he recognized -- 14-year-old Bobby Franks. He was the son of the millionaire Jacob Franks, and a distant cousin of Loeb.

Chosen by chance, he would make the perfect victim for the perfect crime.

Bobby was already acquainted with his killers. He had played tennis with Loeb several times and he happily climbed into the car. Although at their trial, both denied being the actual killer, Leopold was at the wheel and

Loeb was in the back, gripping the murder weapon tightly in his hands when the young boy got into the car. They drove Bobby to within a few blocks of the Franks residence in Hyde Park and then Loeb suddenly grabbed the boy, stuffed a gag in his mouth, and smashed his skull four times with a chisel. The rope had been forgotten. Bobby collapsed onto the floor of the car, unconscious and bleeding badly.

When Leopold saw the blood spurting from Bobby's head, he cried out, "Oh God, I didn't know it would be like this!"

Loeb ignored him, intent on his horrific task. Even though Bobby was unconscious, he stuffed his mouth with rags and wrapped him up in the heavy blanket. The boy continued to bleed for a time and then died on the floorboards of the car.

Bobby Franks

With the excitement of the actual murder concluded, Leopold and Loeb casually drove south, stopped for lunch, and then drove for a little while longer. They had supper as they waited for the sun to go down. Eventually, they ended up near a culvert along the Pennsylvania Railroad tracks. It emptied into a swamp along Wolf Lake.

Leopold put on his hip boots and carried Bobby's body to the culvert. They had stripped off all his clothing and then after dunking his head underwater to make sure that he was dead, they poured acid on his face in hopes that he would be harder to identify. Leopold struggled to shove the naked boy into the pipe and took his coat off to make the work easier. Unknown to the killers, a pair of eyeglasses were in the pocket of Leopold's coat and they fell out into the water when he removed it. This would be the undoing of the "perfect crime."

After pushing the body as far into the pipe as he could, Leopold sloshed out of the mud toward the car, where Loeb waited for him. The killers believed that the body would not be found until long after the ransom money had been received. With darkness falling, though, Leopold failed to notice that Bobby's foot was dangling from the end of the culvert.

They drove back to the city and parked the rental car next to a large apartment building. Bobby's blood had soaked through the blanket and had stained the automobile's upholstery. The blanket was hidden in a nearby yard and the boys burned Bobby's clothing at Leopold's house. They typed out the Franks' address on the already-prepared ransom note. After this, they hurried back to the car and drove to Indiana, where they buried the shoes that Bobby had worn and everything that he had on him that was made from metal, including his belt buckle and class pin from the prep school.

Finally, their "perfect crime" carried out, they drove back to Leopold's home and spent the rest of the evening drinking and playing cards. Around midnight, they telephoned the Franks' home and told Mr. Franks that he could soon expect a ransom demand for the return of his son. "Tell the police and he will be killed at once," they told Franks. "You will receive a ransom note with instructions tomorrow."

The next morning, the ransom note, signed with the name "George Johnson," was delivered to the Franks, demanding $10,000 in old, unmarked $10 and $20 bills. The money was to be placed in a cigar box that should be wrapped in white paper and sealed with wax. After its arrival, the Franks' lawyer notified the police, who promised no publicity.

Meanwhile, Leopold and Loeb continued with the elaborate game they had concocted. They took the bloody blanket to an empty lot, burned it, and then drove to Jackson Park, where Loeb tore the keys out of his stolen typewriter. He threw the keys into one lagoon in the park and the typewriter into another. Later in the afternoon, Loeb took a train ride to Michigan City, leaving a note addressed to the Franks family in the telegram slot of a desk in the train's observation car. He got off the train at 63rd Street, as it returned to the city, and rejoined the waiting Leopold. Andy Russo, a yardman, found the letter and sent it to the Franks.

However, by the time the letter arrived, railroad maintenance men had already stumbled upon the body of Bobby Franks, hanging from the muddy pipe where Leopold had left him. The police notified Jacob Franks and he sent his brother-in-law to identify the body. It was Bobby. The newspapers quickly began putting "extra" editions on the street, alerting the public to the gruesome crime.

Police officers search for clues at Wolf Lake, where Bobby Franks' body was found.

The discovery of the body began one of the largest manhunts in Chicago history. The "perfect crime" almost immediately began to unravel. Despite their "mental prowess" and "high intelligence," Leopold and Loeb were quickly caught. Leopold had dropped his eyeglasses near the spot where the body had been hidden and police had traced the prescription to Albert Coe & Co., who stated that only three pair of glasses with such unusual frames had been sold. One pair belonged to an attorney, who was away in Europe, the other to a woman, and the third pair had been sold to Nathan Leopold.

The boys were brought in for questioning and began supplying alibis for the time when Bobby had gone missing. They had been with two girlfriends, they claimed, "May and Edna." The police asked them to produce addresses for the girls, but the killers could not. Leopold claimed that he had apparently lost the glasses at Wolf Lake during a recent bird-hunting trip. The detectives noted that it had rained a few days before, but the glasses were clean. Could Leopold explain this? He couldn't.

Then, two novice reporters, Al Goldstein and Jim Mulroy, obtained letters that Richard Loeb had written with the stolen typewriter, which had already been found in Jackson Park. The letters matched the type on the ransom note, which was a perfect match for the typewriter that Leopold had "borrowed" from his fraternity house the year before.

Loeb broke first. He said that the murder was a lark, an experiment in crime to see if the "perfect murder" could be carried out. He then denied being the killer and claimed that he had driven the car while Leopold had slashed Bobby Franks to death. Leopold refuted this. Finally, the boys were brought together and admitted the truth. Loeb had been the killer, Leopold had driven the car, but both of them had planned the crime together -- they were both guilty of Bobby Franks' murder.

The people of Chicago, and the rest of the nation, were stunned. It was fully expected that the two would receive a death sentence for the callous and cold-blooded crime.

After the confession, Loeb's family disowned him, but Leopold's father turned to Clarence Darrow, America's most famous defense attorney, in hopes that he might save his son. For $100,000, Darrow agreed to seek the best possible verdict that he could, which in this case was life in prison. "While the State is trying Loeb and Leopold," Darrow said. "I will try capital punishment."

Darrow would have less trouble with the case than he would with his clients, who constantly clowned around and hammed it up in the courtroom. The newspaper photographers frequently snapped photos of them smirking and laughing in court and the public, already turned against them, became even more hostile toward the "poor little rich boys."

Darrow tried every trick in the book and resorted to shameless tactics during the trial. He declared the boys to be insane. Leopold, he said, was a dangerous schizophrenic. They weren't criminals, he railed, they just couldn't help themselves. After this weighty proclamation, Darrow actually began to weep. The trial became a landmark in criminal law. He offered a detailed description of what would happen to the boys as they were hanged, providing a graphic image of bodily functions and physical pain. Darrow even turned to the prosecutor and invited him to personally perform the execution.

Darrow's horrifying description had a marked effect on the courtroom and especially on the defendants. Loeb was observed to shudder and Leopold got so hysterical that he had to be taken out of the courtroom. Darrow then wept for the defendants, wept for Bobby Franks, and then wept for defendants and victims everywhere. He managed to get the best verdict possible out of the case. The defendants were given life in prison for Bobby Frank's murder and an additional 99 years for his kidnapping.

Leopold and Loeb with their famous attorney, Clarence Darrow, who fought valiantly to obtain a sentence of life in prison for the two confessed killers. The trial became a landmark in American criminal law.

Ironically, after all of that, Darrow only managed to get $40,000 of his fee from Leopold's father. He got this after a seven-month wait and the threat of a lawsuit.

Leopold and Loeb were sent to the Joliet Penitentiary. Even though the warden claimed they were treated just like all the other prisoners, they each enjoyed a private cell, books, a desk, a filing cabinet, and even pet birds. They also showered away from the other prisoners and took their meals, which were prepared to order, in the officers' lounge. Leopold was allowed to keep a flower garden. They were also permitted any number of unsupervised visitors. The doors to their cells were usually left open and they had passes to visit one another at any time.

Richard Loeb was eventually killed by another inmate, against whom he had been reportedly making sexual advances. The inmate, James Day, turned on him in a bathroom and attacked him with a razor. Loeb, covered in blood, managed to make it out of the bathroom and he collapsed in the hallway. He was found bleeding by guards and he died a short time later.

It was later discovered that Day had slashed him 56 times with the razor. When Clarence Darrow was told of Loeb's death, he slowly shook his head. "He is better off dead," the great attorney said, "For him, death is an easier sentence."

Leopold lived on in prison for many years and was said to have made many adjustments to his character and some would even say rehabilitated completely. Even so, appeals for his parole were turned down three times. Finally, in 1958, the poet Carl Sandburg, who even went as far as to offer Leopold a room in his own home, pleaded his fourth appeal. Finally, in March of that year, he was released.

He was allowed to go to Puerto Rico, where he worked among the poor and married a widow named Trudi Feldman Garcia de Quevedo, who owned a flower shop. He went on to write a book about his experiences called *Life Plus 99 Years* and continued to be hounded by the press for his role in the "perfect murder" that he had committed decades before. He stated that he would be "haunted" by what he had done for the rest of his life. He died of heart failure on August 30, 1971, bringing an end to one of the most harrowing stories in the history of the city.

"THE GRAY MAN"

Four months before the killer of Marion Parker went to the gallows, another little girl named Grace Budd went missing from her home in New York. She had vanished while en route to a birthday party. Her middle-aged escort, a brief acquaintance known to her family as "Mr. Howard," was also missing. No ransom letters ever arrived. Instead, the family received a letter from her kidnapper that detailed the grisly details of her death.

Grace had not been kidnapped for money. Her abductor had wanted to eat her.

The Budd family first became acquainted with "Mr. Howard" in a way that never raised suspicion. Albert Budd, Grace's hard-working father, made a modest living as a doorman. Money was tight, especially with a growing family. Albert and his wife, Delia, had an 18-year-old son, Edward, and three younger children, Albert, Grace, and Beatrice. To help his father make ends meet, Edward placed an advertisement in the *New York World Telegram*, looking for work. The ad read: "Young man, 18, wishes position in the country," followed by his name and address.

That same afternoon, a nicely-dressed, older gentleman with gray hair and a mustache answered the ad. He came in person, arriving at the Budd home in the Chelsea district of Manhattan. He introduced himself as Frank Howard, a farmer from Long Island who was willing to pay $15 per week to a willing young worker. The family could scarcely believe Edward's good fortune and quickly invited Mr. Howard into the house. After hearing the man's description of his farm, Edward readily accepted the position. "Mr. Howard" promised to return the next week and take not only Edward out to the farm, but his friend, Willie, as well. Howard stressed that he had enough work for both young men.

Grace Budd

Mr. Howard did not return as promised on June 2, which was the following Saturday, but he did send an apologetic telegram, and arrived on Monday, June 5, instead. Impressed by his manners, the Budds greeted him warmly and invited him to stay for lunch. He behaved just like a visiting grandfather, passing out treats and dollar bills to the children. He presented two of the bills to Eddie and Willie and while he said he had a prior engagement, he promised to return that evening to take them to his farm.

Mr. Howard reserved a special surprise for the Budds' oldest daughter, Grace. He told her trusting parents that if they were agreeable to the idea, he wanted to take her to a children's birthday party at the home of his married sister at 137th Street and Columbus Avenue. The Budds readily agreed and Grace left with Howard, holding onto his hand, wearing the white dress that she had worn to church on Sunday morning. The two of them walked off down the street together. The Budds waved goodbye to their little girl and never saw her alive again.

When Grace did not return home that night with Mr. Howard, the Budds were concerned, but not overly worried. They assumed that the party had lasted late and that she had likely spent the night with Mr. Howard's sister. They tried hard to convince themselves of this, even the following morning, when there was still no sign of the girl. Finally, Albert Budd decided to go to the address himself and inquire after his daughter. However, he soon found that the address where Howard's sister supposedly lived did not even exist: Columbus only went as far as 109th. This made his next stop the closest police station, where he was referred to the missing persons bureau and eventually to veteran detective William King.

The detective was suspicious of the situation right from the start. It did not take him long to find that there was no Frank Howard with a farm on Long Island. This also meant that there was no real clue as to the abductor's true identity. The man had covered his tracks well, even going as far as to retrieve the telegram he had sent to the Budds. He had taken it back from them, claiming that he was going to complain to Western Union about it because it had been addressed incorrectly.

Despite the lack of solid clues, King and other members of the bureau started a long and arduous search for the Western Union copy of the telegram. It was the only link that King had to Grace's kidnapper. Three postal clerks spent more than 15 hours sifting through tens of thousands of duplicates with King before they found the one that the man known as Howard had sent. The only clue it provided was that it had been sent from an office in East Harlem. The idea of searching every home in that part of the city was first considered and then abandoned as a physical impossibility.

King then focused on another slim link: a small pail of cheese and a carton of strawberries that Howard had purchased for Mrs. Budd. He told her that they were fresh from the farm. Investigators scoured the East Harlem area until they found the delicatessen where Howard had bought the cheese and they also found the street peddler who had sold him the strawberries. The peddler described the man in detail but could recall nothing else significant about him. Soon, that trail also went cold.

Grace Budd's disappearance started a widespread search through New York City that autumn, particularly after the detective and the Budd family went to the media with the story. Grace's photo appeared on the front page of newspapers and garnered hundreds of tips, leads, and investigation advice from an angry and panicked public. Thousands of circulars were printed and sent out to police departments throughout the United States and Canada, but with no results. The Budds grew more and more despondent as lead after lead went nowhere. Within a few months of Grace's disappearance, even the most dedicated investigators --- with the exception of Will King -- had given up on the case as hopeless.

King was already a legend in New York law enforcement circles when he took on the Grace Budd case and his dogged determination further enhanced his reputation. He was the only investigator who never gave up hope. He thought of Grace and her grieving parents constantly and spent at least part of each day working on the case, following up questionable tips, and making telephone calls. He never let a single lead, no matter how slim, come across his desk that he did not investigate.

Even so, the case went nowhere for the next six years.

At the same time that Detective King was continuing his exhaustive investigation, a man named Albert Fish was arrested in New York and was charged with sending obscene materials, mostly letters, through the mail. In the letters, Fish pretended to be a well-known Hollywood producer and he offered large sums of money to women who might be interested in tying him up and beating him with whips, leather straps, and a variety of other devices. After his arrest, he was committed to the psychiatric ward at Bellevue for a 10-day observation.

Fish remained in Bellevue for nearly 30 days in the winter of 1930. He was polite and cooperative during his stay and the doctors judged him sane, although with sexual problems that they attributed to dementia caused by his advancing age. He was deemed to be harmless and he was released from the hospital into the custody of his daughter, Anna.

Meanwhile, more years had passed in the Grace Budd disappearance. Detective King had not given up hope, but it was starting to look as though the case would never be solved.

Then on November 11, 1934 -- six years after she had been kidnapped -- Mrs. Budd received an unsigned and anonymous letter in the mail. The letter claimed to be from the friend of someone named "Captain John Davis." According to the letter writer, Captain Davis was a seafaring man who, on one of his trips to China, developed a taste for human flesh. He had an intense craving for the flesh of children, an appetite that had come upon him during a famine in the Far East. The letter described in graphic detail how Captain Davis, after returning to New York, had kidnapped and murdered two young boys, had cooked their flesh and had eaten it. After learning from Davis that the flesh of children was "good and tender," the deranged letter writer decided to try it for himself. He had visited the Budd home for lunch and had taken the girl away with him.

Mrs. Budd sobbed hysterically when she read the letter. The writer went into horrific detail about how he had taken Grace to an empty house in Westchester and how he sent her to pick flowers in the garden while he stripped himself naked. He called her into the house and when she saw the grizzled and naked old man, she began to scream. She tried to run away, he wrote, but he caught her, stripped her, and then choked her to death. Then, he dismembered her body and cooked and ate the smaller pieces. Bizarrely, the letter described how Grace had been killed and cut up, but went to extremes to assure Mrs. Budd that she had not been sexually molested in any way. The letter assured the anguished mother, "She died a virgin."

After Mrs. Budd contacted the police about the gruesome letter, investigators went into action, pulling out all stops to find the monster who had written it. The investigation was again led by Detective King, who had deferred his retirement two years earlier so that he could continue to work on the Grace Budd case. King immediately found Mr. Howard's original Western Union telegram blank and there was no doubt about it: the handwriting was the same. "Howard" and the letter writer were one and the same person.

King used a microscope on the letter and discovered an almost indiscernible design on the flap of the envelope. It spelled "N.Y.P.C.B.A." and a quick search through the Manhattan telephone directory revealed the letters to stand for the New York Private Chauffeur's Benevolent Association, headquartered at 627 Lexington Avenue. The association gladly opened its files to Detective King and he spent hours checking the backgrounds and handwriting of their 400 employees. He found nothing that matched.

Undaunted, he called all the employees together and questioned them rigorously. He also added an appeal for any information the drivers might have that could help him with the case. He offered immunity for theft of the letter writing materials and envelopes; all he wanted was to catch the sadistic child killer.

After his appeal to the drivers, King retreated to a private office in the association's headquarters and hoped that his assurances would pay off. A few minutes later, a nondescript man in a chauffeur's uniform named Lee Sicowski knocked on the door. He told Detective King that he had a habit of taking the association's stationary home with him and using it. In fact, Sicowski explained, he had left some of the unused notepaper and envelopes in a room that he had occupied at 622 Lexington. Detectives raced to the rooming house but found nothing there. King then urged Sicowski to think of anywhere else the stationary could have been. Sicowski then remembered that he had also spent some time in a cheap boarding house at 200 East 52nd Street. He might have left some of it there.

This address turned out to be a flophouse and it was there that investigator's determination paid off. The landlady, Mrs. Frieda Schneider, told him that Sicowski's old room was recently occupied by a man who fit "Mr. Howard's" description. His real name was Albert Fish. Carefully, Detective King checked the signature in the room register and he was convinced that the handwriting was the same as that of the letter writer. Fish, unfortunately, had recently left the place, but the landlady told King that he was in the habit of receiving a monthly check from one of his sons. It was always sent to the 200 East 52nd Street address. King was prepared to invest a few more weeks in the hunt for the killer, so he took a room at the top of the stairs, which gave him a view of the entrance and the upstairs and downstairs hallways.

He waited for three days. On December 13, 1934, King received an urgent call from the flophouse. He had left to return to the station and file some paperwork when the landlady called to report Fish was back. When he returned to the house, Mrs. Schneider met him at the door. Fish had come back a half-hour earlier and, to stall him until the detective could get there, she had given him a cup of tea and invited him to sit down. Trying to remain calm, King drew his revolver and walked into the room where Fish waited. He expected a demented killer but what he found was a harmless-looking, white-haired old man with a scraggly mustache and watery blue eyes. He was sipping at a cup of tea. Detective King identified himself and the Fish made no effort to conceal his identity. Then, the detective asked Fish to accompany him to police headquarters for questioning. The seemingly docile old man shocked King by reaching into his pocket and then viciously lunging at him with a straight razor. But he was no match for the detective. King grabbed him by the wrist and twisted it until the razor dropped to the floor. He quickly handcuffed the old man and searched him. To his horror, he found that Fish's pockets were crammed with assorted sharp knives and razors. When he turned the man around to face him, he couldn't help but feel triumphant. "I've got you now," King said.

And a six-year manhunt came to an end.

Albert Fish

After his capture, Fish blamed events in his childhood as the reason for his crimes. He had been abandoned at an early age and placed in an orphanage, where he experienced his first brutal acts of sadism. He had been born in 1870 in the Washington, D.C. area and later married and raised six children. He had limited education and mostly worked as a handyman and a painter. His troubled early life remains a mystery, but according to the testimony of one of his children, his weird and unpredictable behavior began to truly surface in January 1917. It was at this time that his wife ran away with John Straube, a slow-witted handyman who boarded with the Fish family. Fish returned from work one day to find the house deserted and stripped of its furniture.

Mrs. Fish was apparently a bit odd herself. She once returned to her husband with Straube at her side and asked if they could move in with the family. Fish said that she could, but that her lover could not. She understood and sent Straube away. Days later, Fish discovered that his wife had actually hidden Straube in the attic and she was smuggling food up to him. Again, Fish told her that she could stay, but that Straube had to leave. They both departed and the family never saw Mrs. Fish again.

Soon after, Fish became unhinged. When he took his family to their summer home, Wisteria Cottage, in Westchester County, New York, the children would watch, terrified, as he climbed a nearby hill, shook his fist at the sky and repeatedly screamed" "I am Christ!" Pain seemed to delight him, whether inflicting it on himself or others. He took strange pleasure in being whipped and paddled. He encouraged his own children, as well as neighbor children, to paddle his buttocks until they bled, often using a paddle that was studded with inch-and-a-half nails. He also inserted dozens of needles into his body, mostly in his genital region, and burned himself constantly with hot irons and pokers. He began answering classified ads that were placed by widows seeking husbands. His letters --- 46 of them were recovered and entered as evidence at his trial -- were so obscene and vile that the prosecution refused to make them public. Basically, Fish told the lovelorn ladies that he was not as interested in marriage as he was in their willingness to paddle and beat him. None of the women accepted his offers.

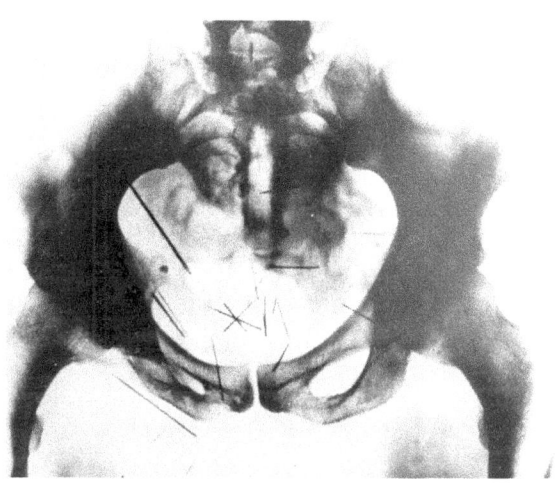

An x-ray of Fish that was taken after his capture showing the dozens of needles that he had inserted into his groin, keeping him in constant pain.

On nights of the full moon, his children later testified, Fish would consume huge quantities of raw meat. Over the years, he collected a great amount of published material on cannibalism and he carried the most gruesome articles with him at all times. Before he committed his first murder, Fish was examined several times by psychiatrists at Bellevue but he was always released and judged "disturbed, but sane."

When, and where, Fish first became a murderer is unknown. He confessed to six killings and referred vaguely to dozens more, although the victims, dates, and places were lost to his hazy memory. He did confess to murdering a man in Wilmington, Delaware; mutilating and torturing to death a mentally retarded boy in New York in 1910; killing a Negro boy in Washington, D.C., in 1919; molesting and killing four-year-old William Gaffney in 1929; and strangling to death five-year-old Francis McDonnell on Long Island in 1934.

But, of course, it was the murder of Grace Budd that finally led the police to Fish's door.

Once in custody, Fish became resigned to his arrest and confessed to succumbing to his "blood thirst" in the summer of 1928. His original victim, he explained, had been intended to be Edward Budd, who had placed the classified advertisement. However, when he got to the Budd house and saw the size of the stocky teenager, he changed his mind and set his sights on the more vulnerable Grace. He freely confessed to kidnapping the girl and taking her to Wisteria Cottage in a place called Worthington Woods, in Westchester County. His recall of the day when he kidnapped the girl was clear after six years, as the old man had probably relived it in his mind over and over again. He had bought a round trip train ticket to Worthington Woods for himself and a one-way ticket for Grace. And he also remembered that when they were changing trains, he had left a bundle behind on the seat. Grace, trying to be helpful, ran back and retrieved it for him. Inside of the bundle were Fish's grisly tools of death: a cleaver, saw and butcher's knife. Grace happily handed them over, never knowing what the old men intended to use them for.

Fish's summer house, Wisteria Cottage, located in Westchester County. It was here that he murdered, cannibalized and buried Grace Budd. Her ghost was reported to linger near the site of the cottage for many years after her death.

After arriving at Wisteria Cottage, Fish sent Grace into the yard while he undressed in one of the rooms on the second floor. When he was naked, he called the little girl into the house. She began to scream when she saw him, threatening to tell her mother what he was doing. Fish grabbed the girl and carried her into a room where he had spread a canvas tarp on the floor. He killed her, choking her and pressing his knee into her chest until there was no breath left in her body. Fish described to the detectives what happened next:

"Then I took a knife and slit her throat. Meantime, I had

picked up a fifty-pound paint pot that holds fifty pounds of lead. I placed that under her head. She had long hair and that soaked up most of the blood. The blood dropped into the pot. After it was there, I threw the pot out. After, I cut her body into three pieces. Cut her head off, through the middle and above the navel. The rest was her legs and the edge of her body."

Fish then told the detectives that he took Grace's severed head to the outhouse, located behind the cottage.

"There was a board that stuck out from the end of the privy that was clean, and I took her shoes, the pair of white shoes, laid them there so they would not be seen by anyone using the toilet, and I laid her head on top of another board so that it would not get down in the muss. Then I took the middle part of her body and legs and shut them behind the door, shut the door to hide them. Then, I went into the yard, wiped the blood off my hands."

Detectives looking over evidence that was discovered at Wisteria Cottage. They later recovered Grace's skeletal remains, still hidden after six years.

Over the next few days, Fish cooked and ate the remaining parts of Grace's body. Detectives reported that he grinned maniacally as he recalled these details. The horrified detectives made their own trip to Wisteria Cottage and recovered the skeletal remains of Grace Budd, which Fish had hidden behind a stone wall.

Detective King finally had his killer, but Fish couldn't stop confessing. He described other murders that he had allegedly committed between 1910 and 1934. Much of what he told police turned out to be false or exaggerated, but he still provided enough details to convince the investigators that he had killed before -- perhaps many times. The detectives were also chilled to discover that Fish had been arrested in the New York area six times since the disappearance of Grace Budd on charges that ranged from petty larceny to vagrancy and sending obscene letters through the mail. Three of the arrests occurred in the three-month period after Grace had been kidnapped and each time the charges against him were dismissed. As for the other arrests, he was released with either a short period of incarceration or a fine. No one ever guessed that the old man was a depraved killer.

Fish was examined by scores of doctors and he relished the notoriety. He described his fetishes and perversions to the fascinated psychiatrists, telling of inserting needles into his scrotum -- X-rays revealed 29 rusty needles in his body -- and inserting wool that was doused with lighter fluid into his anus and setting it on fire. One psychiatrist in particular, Dr. Frederic Wertham, got remarkably close to Fish before and after his trial. He later wrote: "[Fish] looked like a meek and innocuous little old man, gentle and benevolent, friendly and polite. If you wanted someone to entrust your children to, he would be the one you would choose." However, he then went on to describe Fish as the most complex example of a "polymorphous pervert" he had ever known, someone who had practiced every perversion and deviation known to man: from sodomy to sadism, eating excrement, self-mutilation, and murder. Fish even confessed to Wertham that he had carried Grace's ears and nose back to New York with him, wrapped in newspaper. He placed the bundle on his lap as he traveled by train and quivered with excitement as he thought about what was inside.

Like the other examining physicians, Wertham judged Fish to be insane. He said that Fish was a sadist of incredible cruelty, a homosexual, and a pedophile with a penchant for young children. As a self-employed painter, Fish had skulked around basements and cellars for 50 years and preyed on scores of innocent children. He could not begin to guess how many victims the man had claimed. Wertham concluded, "But I believe, to the best of my knowledge, that he has raped one hundred children, at least."

Fish's attorney, James Dempsey, described the needles and the nail-studded paddles to a shocked jury. He told that they were dealing with a tragic mental case. He explained, "We do not have to prove that he is insane. Rather it is up to the state to prove that he is sane."

Dempsey only had one question for the lead psychiatrist for the defense, Dr. Wertham, but that one question about Fish's sanity took more than an hour to read. It was 15,000 words long and covered 45 typewritten pages. Wertham only used three words to reply, "He is insane."

This stunt did nothing to convince the jury that Fish deserved leniency. Whether they believed he was insane or not, they wanted to see the killer punished. He was found guilty and sentenced to the electric chair. Fish was transferred to Sing Sing Prison in 1935 and scheduled to die on January 16, 1935. Dozens of appeals were rejected and as his appointment with the electric chair grew closer, Fish told reporters that he was looking forward to his execution. "It will be the only thrill I have not tried," he said.

On January 16, Fish ate his last meal of a large porterhouse steak and, without aid, entered the death room and walked briskly to the electric chair. He climbed into the seat and helped the guards attach the electrodes to his legs. The reporters and witnesses who were present were aghast at his behavior. He could barely manage to contain his joy at going to a violent death.

Legend claimed that death did not come as quickly as Fish might have liked. When the switch was pulled, according to the story, the first massive jolt of over 3,000 volts failed to kill him. Blue smoke appeared around him, but that was all. It was said that the needles that he had put into his body actually created a short circuit. A story circulated that another prolonged and massive charge had to be sent through his body in order to execute him.

However, none of that was true. Albert Fish died just like every other man who was sent to the electric chair. When the current raced through him, his body surged and his fists clenched. Moments later, the doctor on duty pronounced that Fish -- who at 66-years-old was the oldest man ever executed at Sing Sing -- was dead.

While the old man's corpse was being taken out to the autopsy room, his defense attorney met with reporters. In his hand, he held Albert Fish's final statement, several pages of hand-written notes that the old man had penned in the hours before his death. To this day, the statement has never been revealed. Dempsey told the press, "I will never show it to anyone. It was the filthiest string of obscenities that I have ever read."

As ruthless as Leopold and Loeb were and as deranged as Albert Fish undoubtedly was, the man who kidnapped and murdered Marion Parker was just as cold-blooded and just as insane. Less than four years after the body of young Bobby Franks was found in the waters of Chicago's Wolf

Lake, Marion Parker was lured into danger from a place where she should have been completely safe.

And died a horrible and terrifying death.

KIDNAPPED!

Christmas was coming to Los Angeles in late December 1927. The holiday was only 10 days away when 12-year-old Marion Parker and her twin sister, Marjorie, left home on a Thursday afternoon to attend the Mt. Vernon Junior High School in Arlington, an affluent new suburb on the west side of Los Angeles. Following their usual routine, the girls boarded a streetcar at the corner of Wilton Place and Venice Boulevard.

They had a lot to talk about that morning – excitement over the holiday parties that would take place at school, the Christmas season, time off from school, the days they would spend enjoying their new Christmas presents, and more.

Mt. Vernon Junior High School in the 1920s

The Parker twins were almost always together. They had a brother who was much older and whom both dearly loved, but the special bond that exists between twins was certainly evident between the two girls. Even so, they weren't similar in appearance or in interests. Marjorie loved girlish things, but Marion was a bit of a tomboy. She was never afraid to get dirty, or worried she might be hurt. She had a lot of girl friends at school, but only occasionally played with the neighborhood girls. While Marjorie was playing with dolls, Marion would be off playing with trains or throwing a

A widely-circulated photograph of Marion Parker

football with the local boys. But despite her tomboyish nature and athletic prowess, she was an emotionally delicate child.

Marion never liked to be away from home for long, especially at night. She loved school, parties, and playing with friends, but when evening came, she preferred to be at home with her parents. She was a popular friendly girl, but at age 12, she refused the many invitations that she received for sleepovers.

She was also apprehensive around adults, unless they were neighbors or friends of her parents. It wasn't fear, only a natural shyness that took some time to go away. When she was around those who made her comfortable, she was confident and engaging. Marion would tell jokes, dance to music on the radio or phonograph, and carry on in a silly, childish manner with greater enthusiasm that was shown by her quieter twin sister. Marion laughed merrily at the antics of her favorite movie comedians like Harold Lloyd and Buster Keaton and was delighted by comedy programs on the radio. Marjorie, entertained as much by her sister's happiness as she was by her own, was always less demonstrative than Marion.

Marjorie was her mother's daughter. When not in school, she was content to help out around the house, learning to cook and sew.

Marion, on the other hand, spent her time at the First National Trust and Savings Bank, where her father was an officer. She wandered about the bank, curiously looking around and watching the tellers work. She was not a girl who faded into the background; everyone at the bank knew and liked her – which made what happened in December 1927 all the more tragic.

On the way to school on the morning of December 15, Marion and Marjorie enjoyed the ride on the streetcar, but Marion would later recall, "We were sitting together in one of the car seats when a man drove by the car at about Third Avenue and Venice Boulevard. He smiled at us several times and motioned to us to get off the car and go with him. We looked the other way, but finally saw him turn off at Fourth Avenue."

Earlier that morning, Lorna Littlejohn, a schoolmate of the twins, saw the same man sitting in a small coupe parked at Sixteenth Street and Wilton Place, which was about a block away from the Parker home at 1631 South Wilton Place. Unfortunately, this recollection would come far too late to save Marion Parker.

Just after the noon hour, the same man walked confidently into the office at Mt. Vernon Junior High and approached Mary Holt, the school registrar. When the principal, Cora Freeman, was out, Mrs. Holt took charge as the administrator. She was responsible for making decisions and, by all accounts prior to December 15, she was very strict about the rules, especially when it came to strangers visiting the building and inquiring about the children of whom she was in charge in the principal's absence.

The young man walked into the office around noon, while the children were in their various classrooms enjoying their Christmas parties. In 1927, there were no cameras or locked doors through which visitors could only pass by permission from school personnel. Anyone could simply walk in off the street and enter the main office to see the principal. It was up to the person in charge to meet the visitor, inquire about their business, and give or withhold authorization.

Unfortunately, on this day, the person in charge was Mary Holt.

When the young man walked in, he explained that he worked with Perry Parker at the bank and that Parker had been seriously injured in an automobile accident and he was calling for his daughter. Mrs. Holt was confused – there were two Parker girls at the school. The man explained that Parker wanted his "younger daughter." Of course, there was no "younger daughter," the girls were twins, and Mrs. Holt knew that. This should have alerted her to the fact that something was amiss, but it didn't.

"Do you mean Marion?" she asked the man, who she later described as being very neat and well-dressed with dark, wavy hair.

"Yes. Yes, ma'am, that is her name," he replied.

The stranger didn't know her name. He didn't even know she had a sister. He only knew that Perry Parker had a daughter because he had seen her at the bank where her father worked. But his cool, collected confidence convinced Mrs. Holt that he was telling the truth. He was so well-mannered and calm that even the usually strict Mrs. Holt was won over by his charm. After he suggested that she call the bank and check on his story, she was convinced.

In those days, most people took children's safety for granted. That really wouldn't change much until 1932, when the baby of famous pilot Charles Lindbergh was kidnapped from his New Jersey home. The press called it the "Crime of the Century" and a $50,000 ransom was paid, but for no good purpose. The baby was already dead by the time the money was delivered. A short time later, as police were still looking for the Lindbergh kidnappers, 11-year-old James DeJute, the son of a wealthy contractor, was abducted in Ohio. The ransom note, demanding $10,000 in cash, had a grim warning printed across the top of the page: "Remember Marion Parker."

But in December 1927, neither school officials nor Marion Parker had any obvious reason to fear the friendly young man. Following Holt's instructions, an assistant named Naomi Britton called Marion from her classroom at 12:13 p.m., just as class was about to be dismissed. Holt later told newspaper reporters, "Marion was nervous and excited when I told her that her father had been injured. The news completely broke up a little Christmas party the children were having in their room and Marion had some of the refreshment in her hands when she came into the office. But at once she forgot everything but her father."

In the office, the young man explained to the girl why he was there and told her that he had come to take her to the hospital. He lightly touched her arm when he spoke to her and Marion left with him, showing no hesitation. She had been to the bank so often that perhaps she recognized him when she saw him. We will never know for sure. What is known is that the young man walked her to a roadster that was parked outside and courteously opened the passenger door for her.

It was the last time that anyone saw Marion alive.

Marion had trusted Mrs. Holt's authority when she got into the waiting car that afternoon, just as she had trusted the man who patiently escorted her from the building. Mrs. Holt did not ask Marion if she knew or recognized the man. The stranger had even given Mrs. Holt a name and address, which she failed to write down. She simply assumed that all was well. Even when principal Cora Freeman returned to the school and Mrs. Holt informed her about Perry Parker's accident and that Marion had been picked up by a family friend, all was assumed to be well. Trusting Mrs. Holt's authority and professionalism, Mrs. Freeman never asked her any questions about the severity of the accident or why Marjorie was not alerted, as well. No more was thought about it that day. And, perhaps even stranger, nobody thought it was necessary to tell Marjorie anything at all.

Marjorie waited for her sister outside of the building after school. They also went home on the streetcar together. It was unusual for Marjorie to come home alone, but her parents weren't initially alarmed. Geraldine and Perry assumed that Marion had a good reason for being late. She had likely stayed behind to help her teacher clean up the classroom. Marjorie had not been able to go back into the school and check, or she would have been late for the streetcar. They had no reason to worry, but Perry Parker still decided to call the school office. It was now 4:45 p.m. and it was getting late. It would be dark soon, and he knew Marion did not like to be out alone in the evening. It would be a good idea, he thought, if he just drove over and picked her up himself. He called the number that connected him to the school office. Mrs. Holt answered the phone. Parker greeted her and identified himself.

Mrs. Holt was shocked to hear from Parker and asked how he was feeling. He said that he was fine, assuming that Mrs. Holt was offering a kind greeting. He responded in the same way and then asked if Marion was still at school. It was late and he was going to drive over and pick her up.

Mrs. Holt asked if she had come home with "the man you sent to pick her up." Parker was confused, Mrs. Holt explained the situation and a chill went through Parker as he heard about the family friend, the accident, and Marion's departure from the school several hours before. The cold chill turned to anger and worry.

"I was not in any accident and did not send anyone to pick up Marion from school!" he snapped.

Parker had been home from work the entire day. He had taken time off to spend with his wife – it was his 40th birthday.

Now the Parkers had reason to worry. Panicked and upset, he stammered a quick explanation to his wife. He needed to call the police. Just as he started to dial the telephone, the doorbell rang. He found a Western Union telegram delivery waiting on his doorstep. The wire had been sent from Pasadena two hours earlier. It read: "Do positively nothing till you receive special delivery letter. Marion Parker."

Bewildered and concerned, Parker followed the orders, doing nothing. The next communication he received was not a letter, though, it was another telegram. This one had been sent from Alhambra, California. It read: "Marion secure. Use good judgement. Interference with my plans dangerous." It was signed, "George Fox."

Marion's father, Perry Parker

The name meant nothing to Perry or Geraldine Parker, but it dashed any hope that their daughter had sent the first wire on her own. Parker feared they were dealing with a kidnapper. He was uncertain about what the man wanted, but was terrified to think of their child in a cruel stranger's hands. Prompted by the second telegram, Marjorie recalled the stranger in the dark-colored car who tried to motion to her and her sister on the streetcar that morning. Could he have been the one who took Marion?

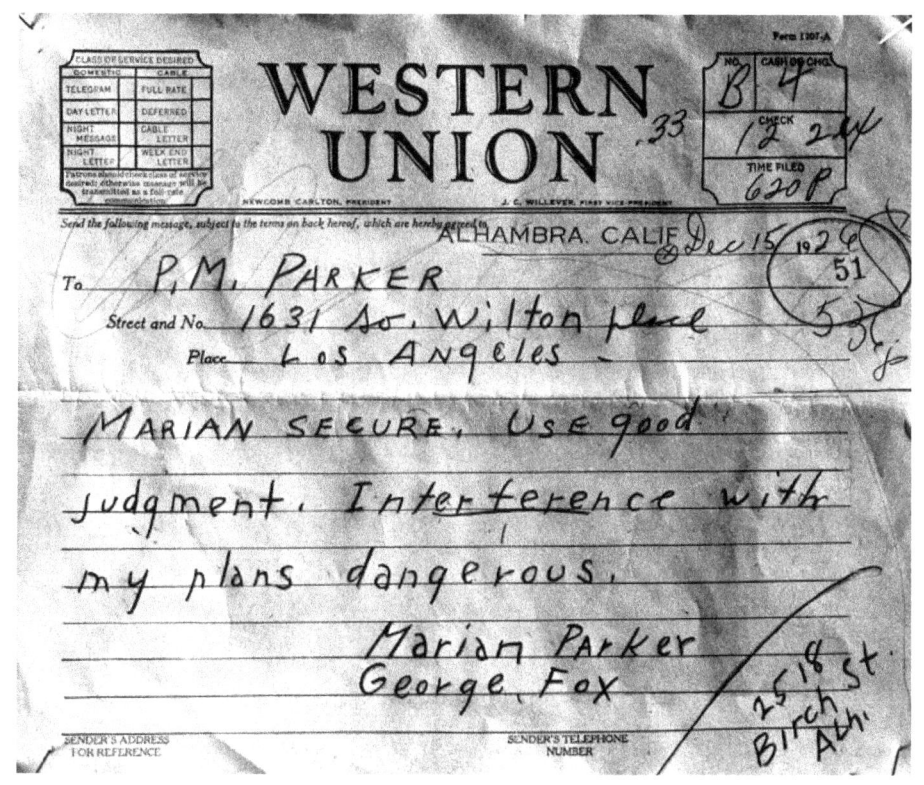

The second telegram that was received at the Parker home after Marion was kidnapped.

Nothing in his life had prepared Parker for anything like this, but his two-and-a-half decades in the banking business had taught him to keep a clear head under pressure. He wasted no time in calling the principal's office at Mt. Vernon Junior High, and then he contacted the police. "I can't understand why anyone would wish to hurt us," he later stated. "We live quietly and I am sure that I have no enemies. We are of moderate means, not the type of family, it seems to me, that would be marked by kidnappers. It is the most puzzling situation that I have ever faced."

Geraldine Parker was naturally distraught over the kidnapping. "All we want, of course, is to get her back safely," she said. "Nothing else matters. And I feel that we shall. We haven't given up hope, by any means. I have an idea that when her abductor realizes the effort that is being made to

Marion, Mrs. Parker and twin sister, Marjorie

find her, he will be frightened and release her. She isn't the type of child that anyone would wish to harm."

A pair of detectives drove out to the house on South Wilton Place. Law enforcement officials quickly circulated a detailed description of the man that Marjorie and Mary Holt described -- who they believed was Marion's kidnapper -- throughout the state of California. It read: "An American, 25 to 30 years of age, 5 feet 8 inches in height, slender build, thin features, smooth-shaven, medium complexion, dark brown hair which is oily and wavy, apparently well-educated, speaks good English, wears a heavy brownish-gray herringbone overcoat, dark gray hat, and dark suit. He is driving a dark-colored coupe or convertible roadster with a spare tire in the rear."

The hastily compiled description would prove to be very close to the mark – with one notable discrepancy. Marion's abductor was much younger than the witnesses believed.

The detectives were still at the Parker home two hours later when a special-delivery letter arrived. It demanded $1,500 for the return of Parker's daughter and warned him -- belatedly -- about the involvement of the police. The note had been written by hand in block letters and was headed by the word "Death," with a Greek letter delta in place of the *D*.

The paltry sum demanded by the kidnapper mystified police detectives. Rarely did a kidnapper ever ask for less than five figures. In addition to the word "Death" at the top of the page, he had signed it with the word "Fate" in oversized letters and then added "George Fox" for good measure.

The letter read:

P.M. Parker:

Use good judgment. You are the loser. Do this. Secure 75-$20 gold certificates – U.S. Currency – 1500 dollars—at once. Keep them on your person. Go about your business as usual. Leave out police and detectives. Make no public notice. Keep this affair private. Make no search. Fullfilling [sic] these terms with the transfer of currency will secure the return of the girl.

Failure to comply with these requests means – no one will ever see the girl again. Except the angels in heaven. The affair must end one way or the other within 3 days. 72 hours. You will receive further notice, but the terms remain the same.

Fate

If you want aid against me ask God, not man.

The kidnapper had included a letter from Marion in the envelope:

Dear Daddy and Mother,

I wish I could come home. I think I'll die if I have to be like this much longer. Won't someone tell me why all this had to happen to me. Daddy please do what the man tells you or he'll kill me if you don't.

Your loving daughter,
Marion Parker

PS. Please Daddy. I want to come home tonight.

It was clearly too late for the Parkers to "leave out police and detectives," but they made a bargain with the Los Angeles Police Department to keep quiet about the kidnapping, releasing no information to the press. That way, with any luck at all, the authorities might have a chance to get a lead on the kidnapper and rescue Marion. Meanwhile, Perry Parker began following the abductor's instructions by collecting $1,500 in twenty-dollar bills.

The ransom demand was strange, almost meaningless, and this puzzled the detectives. Six years earlier, in California's first known kidnapping for ransom, $50,000 was demanded for the safe return of Gladys Witherall. Four years later, in 1925, a $200,000 ransom plot that was aimed at actress Mary Pickford was foiled at the outset, and the would-be kidnappers were sent to prison for 10 years. By 1926, in the wake of evangelist Aimee Semple McPherson's bizarre kidnapping hoax, many Californians had started to regard ransom abductions more as publicity stunts than as actual threats.

But Perry Parker was taking no chances with his daughter's life. He would pay the demand, ignoring the advice of detectives, if only "Fate" or "George Fox," or whatever his name was, would tell him when and where.

There was no sleep for Perry and Geraldine on Thursday night, as they attempted to convince each other that Marion would be fine. Parker paced the floor, waiting for the telephone to ring. On Friday, December 16, Parker went to work, as "Fate" had ordered him to do, and returned home again that afternoon to find there was still no word about Marion.

The police had visited Marion's school and questioned Mary Holt. They had a description of the kidnapper, but could not share it with the press. As for the dark automobile, it could be anywhere. Los Angeles was already a city on wheels, with thousands of cars on the streets. Without a license number, the police could never hope to trace one particular automobile.

Three times on Friday afternoon the telephone rang at the Parker house, but there was no one on the line when Perry answered. There was only the hiss of an open line for a moment, followed by a click, and a dial tone. Wrong numbers? Or were the Parkers being tested by the kidnapper?

At 8:00 p.m., the telephone rang for the fourth time. This time, when Parker picked up, a male voice said, "I'll call back in five minutes."

Nearly a half hour passed before the telephone rang again. Parker, his nerves pushed to their limits, immediately snatched the receiver. It was the same voice, asking him if he had the

Perry and Geraldine Parker, with Marion's grandmother, at left. Their lives following Marion's death were filled with overwhelming grief.

money. He did. Parker was told to leave the house immediately and alone, drive north on Wilton Place to Tenth Street, turn right onto Tenth, and park on Gramercy. If he obeyed these instructions to the letter, someone would approach his car and trade his daughter for the cash.

The banker followed the orders, carrying the thick stack of cash in his pocket, and taking the route that had been dictated by the caller. He parked on Gramercy, dimmed his headlights, and waited for the kidnapper to arrive. After waiting for a half hour, desperately watching each passing car and staring at every pedestrian that passed him by, Parker began to worry that something had gone wrong. He sat and waited until 11:45 p.m. before he finally gave up and drove home.

It was only when he arrived back at his house that Parker learned that he had been followed by the police. They had his home staked out, prepared for anything. Detectives believed that if they could spot the kidnapper when he retrieved his ransom, they could trail him to his hideout – or, if Marion was freed on the street, they would arrest him on the spot. Several carloads of officers had followed Parker to the meeting spot, surrounding the area, and the kidnapper quickly realized the trap and did not show himself.

The botched ransom exchange had shaken things up considerably, and it was no longer possible to keep the story out of the newspapers. News of the abduction broke on Saturday morning, with a front-page story in the *Los Angeles Times*. In the era of Leopold and Loeb, the press had another chilling story to tell and it was widely reported across the country. Nearly every paper had it on the front page – a child was in the dangerous clutches of a kidnapper and America was on alert.

In the *Times* story, Marion was described as 12-years-old, four feet six inches tall, and weighing 100 pounds. She had brown eyes, an olive complexion and bobbed hair. When she disappeared, she was wearing an English print dress of mixed colors, brown Oxford sport shoes and stockings, a sweater vest with no collars or lapels with a blue back and blue sleeves, and no hat.

The story also offered the description that Mary Holt had given to the police, adding that he was driving a dark-colored coupe or roadster with a spare tire in rear. There were also confident quotes from Chief of Detectives Herman Cline, who stated that Marion's safety was the major concern of the department. It was only a matter of time, he said, before she was returned home and her kidnapper was apprehended.

Cline, nicknamed "Hard-Boiled Herman," was a classic 1920s L.A. detective – the kind of man who influenced later movie portrayals of tough-guy cops. He was hard as nails and a no-nonsense sort and had a habit of steamrolling through cases to successful conclusions. Taking a keen interest in the plight of Marion Parker, he stated that scores of detectives had been shifted from their other duties to focus on the Parker case. He was receiving full cooperation from all detective and police forces in the Los Angeles area, including working closely with fellow Chief of Detectives George Contreras. Contreras, like Cline, was a tough character with an inside knowledge of the streets of L.A. With these two men on the case, everyone believed, Marion's rescue was only a matter of time.

The police stated that they still believed that someone close to the Parker family had perpetrated the kidnapping. They based this on the fact that the stranger knew that Parker worked at the bank, that he had a daughter, and where she went to school. The Parkers, however, could not comprehend that as a possibility. They couldn't believe that anyone they knew would put their daughter in peril.

The police knew otherwise. Even so, Herman Cline insisted that Marion would be returned unharmed and that the kidnapper would be caught. He was sure all would be well. Perry Parker was still terrified. "The money means nothing," he told reporters. "All I want to know is that Marion is not harmed and to have her sent back to us. The waiting is terrible, and it seems as if time would never pass. Surely we will hear something before the day is over."

Perry Parker did hear something. As stunned and upset as he had been to learn that the police had clumsily followed him to the ransom drop, he was no more upset than Marion's kidnapper. On Saturday morning, a second special-delivery envelope arrived at the Parker home, with two letters folded inside. The first was again headed "Death" with the now familiar Greek *D* and an arrow pointing down to the next line down: *"Death approaching nearer each and every hour."* The letter itself read:

P.M. Parker:

When I asked you over the phone to give me your word of honor as a Christian and honest businessman not to try and trap or tip the police you didn't answer – Why? – Because those two closed cars carefully followed your car north on Wilton to 10th and then proceeded to circle the block on Gramercy, San Marino, Wilton and 10th. I knew and you knew – what for? One was a late model Buick and the other had disc wheels. Then later, only a few minutes I saw a yellow Buick police car speeding toward your neighborhood. Of course you don't know anything about these facts – and that is sarcasm!

Mr. Parker, I'm ashamed of you! I'm vexed and disgusted with you! With the whole damn vicinity throbbing with my terrible crime you try and save the day by your simple police tactics. Yes, you lied, and schemed to come my way, only far enough to grab me and the girl too. You'll never know how you disappointed your daughter. She was eager to know that it would only be a short while and then she would be free from my terrible torture and then you mess the whole damn affair.

Your daughter saw you, watched you work, and then drove away severely broken hearted because you couldn't have her in spite of my willingness – merely because you, her father, wouldn't deal straight for her life.

You're insane to betray your love for your daughter, to ignore my terms, to tamper with death. You remain reckless, with death fast on its way.

How can the newspapers get all these family and private pictures unless you give them to them? Why all the quotations of your own self, Marion's twin sister, her aunt and school chums? All this continues long after you received my strict warnings.

Today is the last day. I mean Saturday, December 19-year-1927 [sic].

I have cut the time to two days and only one more time will I phone you. I will be two billion times as cautious, as clever, and as deadly from now on. You have brought this on yourself and you deserve it and worse. A man who betrays his love for his daughter is a second Judas Iscariot – many times more wicked than the worst modern criminal.

If by 8 PM today, you have not received my call – then – hold a quiet funeral service at your cemetary [sic] without the body – on Sunday, the 18th – only God knows where the body of Marion Parker would rest in this event. Not much effort is needed to take her life. She may pass out before 8 PM. So I could not afford to call you and ask you for your $1500 for a lifeless mass of flesh.

I am base and low but I won't stoop to that depth, especially to an ungrateful person.

When I call, if I call, I'll tell you where to go and how to go. So if you go don't have your friends following. Pray to God for forgiveness for your mistake last night. Become honest with yourself and your blood. If you don't come in this good, clean, honest way and be square with me – that's all.

Fate – Fox

If you want aid against me ask God, not man.

There was a note enclosed with the kidnapper's angry letter:

Dear Daddy and Mother:

Daddy, please don't bring anyone with you today. I'm sorry for what happened last night. We drove right by the house and I cried all last night. If you don't meet us this morning you will never see me again.

*Love to all,
Marion Parker*

The angry tone of the letter had Perry Parker fearing the worst. He had not, as the abductor claimed, asked the police to follow him to the aborted meeting. However, there was no way for him to let the kidnapper know this. He was frantic with worry and contacted Chief of Detectives Cline, insisting that he be allowed to act alone. He did not want another botched ransom drop to result in his daughter being hurt, or worse, killed.

Cline was skeptical about allowing Parker to go alone to meet the kidnapper. Parker was a simple, hardworking family man who had never dealt with the criminal element before. He had no idea how to deal with this kind of situation, and didn't know what was best. Even so, Cline understood the father's concern. He realized that it was something that Parker needed to do and the detective relaxed his tough demeanor and gave Parker his wish.

But would Parker hear from the kidnapper? Had the actions of the previous night so angered the kidnapper that he intended to harm Marion? Parker must have felt some small bit of relief later that afternoon when a second special-delivery envelope arrived. It contained two more letters. The first one, written by the kidnapper, had a weary, but patient, tone. It seemed that his initial letter had allowed him to blow off some steam. The second letter was more understanding, although with Marion still missing, there was still an ominous undercurrent. The letter read:

P.M. Parker:

Please recover your senses. I want your money rather than to kill your child. But so far you give me no other alternative.

Of course you want your child but you'll never get her by notifying the police and causing all this publicity. I feel however, that you started the search before you received my warning, so I am not blaming you for the bad beginning.

Remember the 3-day limit and make up for this lost time. Dismiss all authorities before it is too late. I'll give you one more chance. Get that money the way I told you and be ready to settle.

I'll give you a chance to come across and you will or Marion dies.

Be sensible and use good judgment. You can't deal with a master mind like a common crook or kidnapper.

Fox – Fate

If you want aid against me ask God, not man.

The second note in the envelope was not from Marion this time. Oddly, it was a second letter from the kidnapper. It once again bore the familiar "Death" with a Greek letter *D* heading and the author seemed determined to make his point. Also, through greed or simple stupidity – this issue has puzzled crime writers for years – he either escalated the ransom or merely confused $20 bills with $100 notes. He wrote:

P.M. Parker:

Fox is my name. Very sly you know. No traps, I'll watch for them.

All the inside guys, even your neighbor Isadore B., know that when you play with fire there is cause for burns. Not W.J. Burns [a reference to a leading private detective of the era] and his shadowers either. Remember that.

Get this straight! Remember that life hangs by a thread and I have a Gillette ready and able to handle the situation.

Do you want the girl or the 75-- $100 gold certificates, U.S. currency? You can't have both and there's no other way out. Believe this and act accordingly. Before the day is over I'll find out how you stand.

I'm doing a solo, so figure on meeting the terms of Mr. Fox, or else.

Fate

If you want aid against me ask God, not man.

And there was still one more letter to come. When this one arrived, it was again headed by "Death," but this time, a large, hand-scrawled line also noted, "Final Chance Terms." The badly-numbered note read:

1. Have $1500 = 75 – 20 dollar gold certificates – U.S. currency.
2. Come alone and have no other following or knowing the place of the meeting.
4. Bring no weapons of any kind.
3. Come in the Essex coach license number – 544-995. Stay in the car.

The "Final Chance Terms" letter – the last that Parker would receive from the "Fox"

If I call, your girl will still be living. When you go to the place of the meeting you will have a chance to see her – then without a second's hesitation you must hand over the money. (The slightest pause of misbehavior on your part at this moment will be tragic)

Seeing your daughter and transferring the currency will take only a moment. My car will then move slowly away from yours for about a block. You wait and when I stop I will let the girl out. Then come and get her.

Don't blunder. I have certainly done my part to warn and advise you.

Fate

If you want aid against me ask God, not man.

Perry Parker was determined not to let anything get in the way of his daughter's rescue, but by the time that he read this letter, the kidnapper had already sealed the fate of Marion Parker – and his own. A few minutes after the little girl had written the second letter to her parents, the kidnapper killed her.

He later stated that he fully intended to keep his promise to Perry Parker and deliver the girl in exchange for the ransom, but something came over him and he was "completely gripped" by the "intention to murder." Grabbing a dish towel from the kitchen, he returned to Marion, who was tied to a chair, and then "gently placed the towel about her neck and explained that it might rest her head." Then, he suddenly "pulled the towel about her throat and applied all my strength to the move. She made no audible noise except for the struggle and heaving of her body during the period of strangulation, which continued for about two minutes."

The exertions left the young man sweaty and disheveled, so he washed his face, combed his hair, and straightened his clothing. He then left the building where he lived and went to the nearest drugstore, where he purchased rouge, lipstick, and face powder. He told the salesgirl that he was buying the cosmetics for his sister. He casually walked back to his apartment and began the most gruesome aspects of the crime.

He stripped off Marion's clothing, carried her body into the bathroom, and laid her face down in the bathtub, with her head over the drain. With a large butcher's knife from the kitchen, he slit her throat and then he turned on the water in the tub. As the blood drained from her body, he went to the refrigerator and made a snack of sardines and crackers. He slowly ate as the water did its work.

A little while later, he returned to the bathroom. He stripped down to his undershorts and went to work on the corpse using a set of "improvised surgical instruments" – the butcher's knife, a pocket knife, a kitchen fork, an icepick, and a package of razors. He began -- in the words of Richard Cantillon, who later worked on the kidnapper's defense team at trial and wrote a powerful account of the case -- by effecting "a disjunction from the body of the arms at the elbows and the legs at the knees. Then he cut an opening in the abdomen, removing the viscera. The odor from the entrails made him sick to his stomach and he vomited into the toilet bowl."

Fighting his nausea, he went into the living room and stood by the open living room window for a few minutes. After his stomach settled, he went back to the bathroom and wrapped the viscera in a "thick newspaper bundle." The body now had to be butchered. He began sawing through the dead girl's backbone and as he did, the upper portion of the body began jerking about violently, nearly flailing out of the tub. The kidnapper was momentarily shocked, but had spent time working in a slaughterhouse and knew how chickens behaved after being decapitated and decided the reaction had something to do with the spinal cord being severed. He ignored it.

After the blood was wiped from the skin and washed from the hair, the killer lifted the torso from the tub and wiped it dry. He gathered every towel that he had in the apartment and stuffed them into the cavity of the corpse. He needed it to remain rigid. Satisfied, he gently cradled the head to protect it from being disconnected and carried the torso into the living room and placed it upright on the couch. The killer wrapped her severed limbs in newspaper and placed them next to the body. As he did so, Marion's glassy, dead eyes seemed to watch him as he walked in and out of the room. The kidnapper was oblivious to the grim tableau.

On his hands and knees, he scrubbed the bathroom floor, washed out the tub, and took a warm bath. Once he was dressed, he "picked up the cosmetics and with the ineptitude of an amateur beautician, applied the rouge, lipstick, and face powder to the dead face. He slipped her school dress over the head and torso, carefully pinning it so it would remain in place and cover the wound on the throat." As a final touch, he sewed open her eyelids, then "brushed and fixed Marion's hair into a ponytail, held in place with her hair ribbon, tied in a neat bow."

"The entire effect," Cantillon wrote, "was quite lifelike."

The chilling "Final Chance Terms" letter was followed by a telephone call. Around sundown, the telephone rang. It was the same male voice, reminding Parker that his daughter's life was hanging in the balance. He had one final chance to pay the ransom. If he failed, or if the police followed him to the scene, Marion would die. The banker stated that he understood the terms, so he was startled when the line suddenly went dead.

It was 7:15 p.m. before the kidnapper called back. The time had come, he told Parker. He was to leave the house immediately and drive north on Wilton Place to Fifth Street. He was to turn right at the intersection, drive another three blocks to the east, and park at the corner of Manhattan Place. His car was known and would be recognized.

Parker left immediately. As he drove, he checked his rearview mirror, nervously hoping that the police would keep their word and not follow him this time. He had pleaded with detectives, knowing that his daughter's life was in great danger.

When he reached the rendezvous point, he switched off his engine and waited in the darkness. Manhattan Place was a residential neighborhood, mostly dark. Streetlights were few and far between in 1927.

It was nearly 8:15 p.m. when the headlights flashed in Parker's rearview mirror and the dark roadster pulled up beside him. Parker recognized it as the same car that had passed by without stopping a few minutes earlier. The driver leaned across the front seat, and in the dim light Parker could see that he was disguised. He had some sort of cloth masking his lower face, like a bandit in a western film.

A sawed-off shotgun nosed across the roadster's windowsill, the two muzzles aimed at Parker's face. "You see this gun"" the muffled voice of the stranger asked.

"I see it," Parker replied.

"Well, did you bring the money?"

Parker took the thick stack of bills from the pocket of his overcoat. "Here it is," he said, holding it up so that the kidnapper could see it.

"Give it to me," the masked man ordered him.

Parker hesitated. "Where's Marion?" he asked.

"Right here," the kidnapper replied," she's asleep."

As proof, he reached down with the hand not holding a shotgun and lifted a blanket. Parker could see his daughter's face, a pale shape in the shadows. Her eyes were open, but she did not speak. The kidnapper quickly covered her up again.

"All right, now the money," he growled.

Parker handed over the money and asked if the man intended to give back his daughter.

The kidnapper answered, "Yes, just as I said. Wait here just a minute."

"How far are you going?" asked Parker.

"Not far."

The roadster eased forward, just a couple of hundred feet. The brake lights flashed on. In the pale light, Parker saw the passenger door swing open and saw a bundle fall out onto the ground. The door then slammed shut and the automobile sped off into the night.

Fearing a trick, Parker edged his car forward, peering over the dashboard to look at the place where the roadster had stopped. At first, he thought the object lying next to the curb was a bag of trash, but then he saw his daughter's pallid face and realized that she was still wrapped in a blanket.

Parker braked but left his engine running as he jumped out of the car, stumbling in his haste. He fell down, scraping his hands on the pavement, and then scrambled toward where his daughter was still lying prone against the curb. He called her name, but she did not stir.

Her eyes were open, but there was something dull and flat about them. There was something wrong with her eyelashes too, though he could not be sure at first just what it was.

"Marion?" he called, his voice quavering.

As he reached for his daughter, he whispered her name; still no response. It struck him that she seemed too small, somehow. At a glance, he thought perhaps her knees were drawn up to her chest, from sitting on the car seat. But as he picked her up, he realized that he was wrong.

Part of his daughter was missing. She was dead and she had been cut into pieces.

On the verge of a complete collapse, Perry Parker found a telephone and he called the Chief of Detectives Herman Cline. Within minutes, the greatest manhunt in the city's history had begun.

HUNTING "THE FOX"

LAPD Detective George Contreras was one of the officers who reached the scene at Manhattan Place "seven or eight minutes after the call came into headquarters." He found Perry Parker standing beside his car, still running, exactly where he had left it.

Parker's agonized cries had alerted nearby residents, many of whom came out and comforted him. Several of them were still surrounding him when Contreras arrived. Grown men were in tears, he later recalled, and Parker was too stunned to cry.

Contreras later testified: "I walked up to him and asked him where his little girl was, and he said, 'There she is, sitting in the car. Go and look at her. God bless her little heart.' And he could talk no more, and this friend of his had to take him away. So, I immediately went over to the car, and the little girl was sitting there with her little head leaned over to the right, and the first thing that attracted my attention was the thread that was fastened over each eyelid and across the forehead and right back over the head and down around the neck, and sewed onto a white piece of linen that went around the neck. I lowered the little cloth, and there was a cut there, so I did not touch it any more, on account of getting finger marks on it."

He added: "She had, as I say, this linen around her neck and a sweater on, buttoned up, and sat in that position. I made an examination and lifted the body up, and told Inspector Taylor that all of the body wasn't there. He came over and made an examination, and talked to Parker and searched the automobile, and searched the block. And when the coroner came, I carried the body out of the automobile and put it in the wagon, and we came on down to the morgue with it."

Dr. A.F. Wagner was waiting to perform the first phase of the autopsy, with *Los Angeles Times* photographer George Watson on hand to photograph the corpse. Dr. Wagner had no difficulty identifying the body. He had lived next door to the Parker family for the last four years. It was just after 9:00 p.m. when he began his postmortem examination, which he later described during the killer's trial.

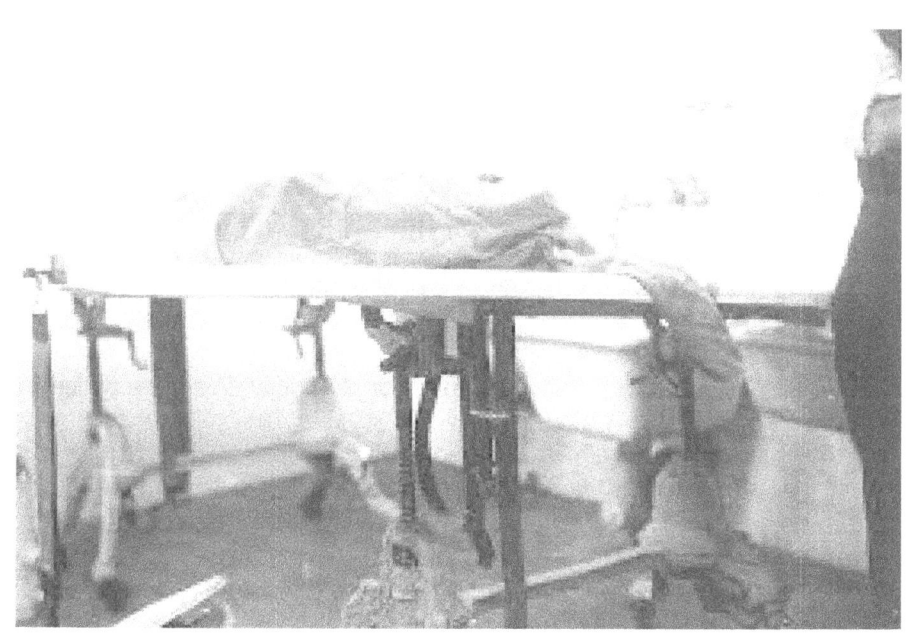

The body of Marion Parker at the morgue

Wagner testified: "On the first evening, I found part of the body, consisting of the head, the trunk down to an inch and a half below the navel, with the arms intact, but the forearms disarticulated at the elbows. I examined that part of the body. I found there was also a cut made by a knife on the left – on the top of the left shoulder. This cut was two and a half inches long. There were a very few superficial marks around this cut, especially between the cut and the head, which I could not determine at the time as to their cause. There were merely very superficial cuts. There were no other marks

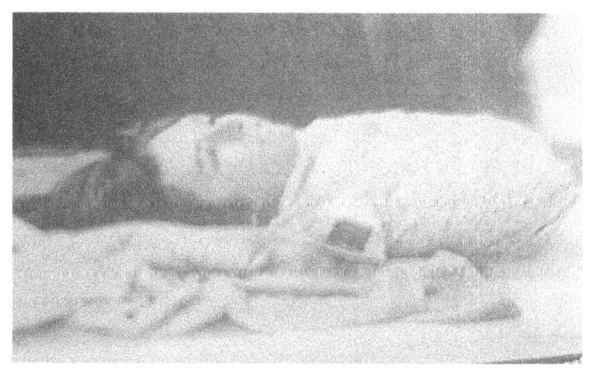

The tragic victim was photographed by a newspaper photographer for the postmortem.

upon that part of the body at all. There was no discoloration to the face. There were no contusions about the neck."

Before he opened the torso, Dr. Wagner noted that the eyelids had been stitched open. He reported, "I examined the organs of the body, the lungs and heart, the trachea, and I found everything without any evidence of contusion or blow. That included also the stomach, the liver, kidneys, which were all intact, all in perfectly normal, healthy shape."

In addition to the towels that had been stuffed into Marion's abdominal cavity, Dr. Wagner also extracted part of a man's shirt, with the name "Gerber" printed inside of the collar. The name meant nothing, but no one knew it at the time, and this false clue would initially divert the police from the true identity of the kidnapper.

Meanwhile, the killer was busy looking for supper. His activities of the night had caused him to work up an appetite. He dropped off his car at Ninth and Grand and walked over to the Leighton Café, on Broadway between Fifth and Sixth Streets. He used one of the $20 bills that Perry Parker had given him to pay for his food. On a whim, he spoke to the cashier when he was leaving the diner. "You would be surprised if you knew who I was," he said. He later told detectives that he wished that he could have seen the girl's face when she found out. He added, "I'll bet she got a thrill."

His hunger satisfied, the killer left his car in a public lot and caught a streetcar back to his apartment, where he promptly went to sleep.

A short time later, a patrolman spotted the roadster, which matched the description of the car used in the ransom drop, and questioned the parking lot attendant. He was told that the driver, a young dark-haired man, had promised to return for the car on Sunday. Fingerprints that were lifted from the windshield turned out to be a match for those found on the ransom notes. The automobile, it turned out, had been stolen from a doctor in Kansas City in early November.

Would the driver return? Swearing members of the press to secrecy, detectives staked out the car and waited for the suspect to come for it.

Within hours of the body's discovery, the people of Los Angeles were gripped with terror. Their fears were enflamed by the sensational newspaper headlines and melodramatic radio broadcasts. The Sunday *Times* carried the headline "Kidnapped Child Slain by Fiend," with Marion's portrait in the center, flanked by details of the "gigantic search" for her killer.

The following day, parents kept their children home from school, while the police spread the word to the public, appealing to them to watch out for "suspicious characters" and to immediately contact the authorities if they saw anything unusual.

The rest of Marion's body, the sections of which were wrapped in newspaper, were found in a nearby park. As far as the police could determine, they had been thrown out of the killer's car.

Things were bad, but there was worse to come.

William Britton was miles away from his home in suburban Downey, strolling through Elysian Park in Chavez Canyon – now home to the Los Angeles Dodgers -- when he discovered four newspaper-wrapped parcels scattered along the road. Curious, he opened one of them and found a small human arm, severed at the elbow. Startled, he rushed to call the police. When detectives arrived, they found the other parcels contained a second arm and two lower legs.

About an hour later and 150 yards farther east, two boys hiking in the woods found another package lying in a gully, where it had rolled after it was tossed from the window of the killer's automobile. Wrapped in more stained newspaper was the pitiful remainder of Marion's body, truncated at the waist and the knees.

Investigators found tire tracks on the muddy shoulder there, when the killer had pulled over to the side. They made a cast, which matched the tires of the roadster then under watch in the parking lot at Ninth and Grand. So far, the young man had not returned to claim it.

That Sunday morning, the police were back at Manhattan Place. A woman named Margaret Root had found a suitcase standing in the gutter in front of her house, a block from the spot where Marion's body had been dumped by "Fox." The suitcase was cheaply made, imitation leather. Inside it police found one clean towel, two bloody newspapers, a writing tablet that appeared to match the two notes written by Marion to her father, and a spool of black thread that was identical to the stitching in Marion's eyelids.

Dr. Wagner was waiting at the morgue when the rest of Marion's corpse arrived. As he later testified in court: "On the morning of the next day, the other parts of the body had been brought in, in separate pieces, each arm, and each leg from the knee down, and also the other parts of the body, ranging from an inch and a half below the navel down to the knees. I examined these parts very closely. I could find no evidence of contusion or abrasion or scratches upon the ankles, except very slight, superficial abrasions. The lower part of the body that was brought in contained the genital organs, which were all intact." Despite the absence of any apparent mortal wounds to the head of torso, Dr. Wagner logically concluded that his young neighbor had suffered a "violent homicidal death."

The horrific crime invited all kinds of psychiatric speculation about the killer's motives. Newspaper reporters went looking for any expert that would speak with them and while most were far removed from the crime scene, their statements were splashed across the front pages of newspapers around the country. One of the first to be interviewed was Dr. Paul Bowers, a professor of legal medicine at Loyola College and the former superintendent of the Indiana Hospital for the Insane. He believed that Marion's murder was the work of a sexual sadist, the ransom demand to disguise the fact that the crime was "planned and carried out for the gratification of an abnormal sexual impulse." The killer was "not a moron," Bowers said, but rather "more or less conventionally well-educated."

Los Angeles psychiatrist Victor Parkin agreed, suggesting that the paltry sum of just $1,500 for the ransom was because it "would just about cover his expenses in making his escape." According to Dr. Parkin, the typical sadist possessed a "high degree of cunning and egotism." Marion's killer might well appear normal in everyday life, perhaps holding employment as a trusted office worker.

Dr. Joseph Catton, a psychiatrist in San Francisco, generally agreed with his colleagues, profiling a killer that had an "emotional disturbance which probably affects his sex life." At the same time, though, he warned against believing the man was legally insane. Whoever he was, Dr. Catton had no sympathy for him. He told a reporter, "Society's impulse to do away with this type of offender should be acted on... I feel that this case cries out for vengeance."

At the same time that the killer was enjoying a movie in a local theater, the LAPD was receiving their first false lead in the case. A tailor in Alhambra, S.A. Nemeth, told detectives that two men and a woman had entered his shop on Saturday morning, around eleven o'clock. One of the men "resembled" Marion's still-unidentified killer. He carried an overcoat and two loose buttons, and asked Nemeth to sew them back on. The tailor noted "dark spots which looked like bloodstains" on the coat, but when he tried to remove them, the owner ordered him to leave the stains alone and just reattach the buttons. Nemeth's description of the second man and the woman were vague, but detectives were impressed with his report, which, of course, got them no closer to the killer.

In the days that followed, the account was forgotten as more suspects were discovered. There seemed to be no shortage of them. One of those questioned on Sunday was the 25-year-old son of a local physician, "known in the past to have committed offenses against young girls." Detectives said that he was in a position to know "intimate details" about the Parker family life, but he came up with an airtight alibi and was quickly released.

With the kind of publicity that the case was getting in the newspapers, LAPD detectives were anxious to make an arrest. On Monday morning, the *Los Angeles Times* dramatically reported, "Swooping down from the sky, airplanes carrying Los Angeles detectives last night halted an east-bound bus at Las Vegas, Nevada, and arrested Lewis D. Wyatt as a suspect in the Marion Parker kidnapping and murder case. Two airplanes carrying the Los Angeles officers headed off the bus just as it came to a stop in Las Vegas to take on gas. They removed Wyatt and escorted him at once to the police station, where he was fingerprinted and photographed."

The story made great headlines, but the LAPD could have put the money they paid to charter two airplanes to better use since Wyatt ended up having no connection at all to the Parker case. His purchase of a ticket to Terre Haute, Indiana, using two $20 gold certificates had been all that had triggered his arrest. No one bothered to check and see if the serial numbers on his bills matched those on the list of ransom bills. Wyatt was briefly detained at the Clark County Jail, but the lawmen found him too old and "too stocky" to be their quarry, and he was soon on his way back to Terre Haute.

In Pasadena, Joe Montgomery, 21, had a tougher time with the police, but he brought the trouble on himself. Montgomery was out riding his motorcycle with a female friend when he approached an LAPD roadblock on the outskirts of the city and decided not to stop. Police gave chase and even fired gunshots at him, but Montgomery eluded them by cranking up his motorcycle to speeds of as high as 68 miles per hour. Somewhere along the way, he ditched his date, but officers caught up with him at 2:30 a.m., when he visited Pasadena Emergency Hospital to have a bullet removed from his foot.

On that Sunday, detectives questioned five suspects who "resembled" the killer, but all of them were released. The weekend dragnet had come up empty.

The Parker family home before the kidnapping and the crush of publicity that overwhelmed the family.

While the LAPD was chasing leads, rewards began to be offered for information that would lead to the arrest of Marion's killer. City and county officials both offered rewards of $5,000. Warner Brothers' radio station, KFWB, announced pledges of more than $20,000 in listener contributions toward a reward fund. Station KMIC in Inglewood received promises of contributions totaling near $4,000. At Angelus Temple in Echo Park, famed evangelist Aimee Semple McPherson – who had faked her own kidnapping the previous year -- also sent out a plea to her followers. William Bonelli, president of the L.A. city council, pledged $5,000 toward the killer's arrest, a sum that was instantly matched by Sidney Graves from the county board of supervisors. The reward fund eventually reached nearly $100,000.

Well-wishers and curiosity-seekers flocked to the Parker home. Some wanted to help in any way that they could, sharing the crushing grief of the family, while others just wanted to try and be a part of the most sensational murder case of the moment. Late on Monday afternoon, Mr. Parker asked the police to rope off the block surrounding his home. More than 25,000 people had gathered on the street and the constant voices, car engines and honking horns was fraying Mrs. Parker's already jangled nerves.

While all of this was taking place, the object of all of their attention was preparing to get out of town. The police had narrowly missed him at his apartment and he later claimed that he talked his way out of an arrest, but no one knows if that really happened. What is known – thanks to an eyewitness account – is that around 5:00 p.m. on Sunday, he rode a streetcar to Hollywood Boulevard and Western Avenue to look for a car that would get him out of town. He had decided not to return to the stolen roadster – unaware that it was being watched by the police – and found a Hudson that was driven by Frank Peck, a Los Angeles dealer in wholesale building supplies. The killer watched Peck drop off his wife in front of a shop on Hollywood Boulevard, and start looking for a place to park. The killer quickly opened the passenger door and slipped into the car, a pistol in his hand. He forced his way into the driver's seat, drove a short distance, and then made Peck get out of the car. Peck did as he was told and watched the Hudson vanish into the night.

The killer left Los Angeles on Ventura Boulevard, drove overnight, and ended up in San Francisco. He checked into the Herald Hotel, registering as "Edward J. King" of Seattle, on Monday afternoon, and spent the night in room 402. He only planned to stay one night and then he would head north.

He slept well that night, not knowing that, by now, the police knew his name, but they had no idea where to find him.

The killer had left Los Angeles in chaos. Another threatening letter for the Parker family had been found on Sunday afternoon, stashed in a fire alarm box at the corner of Hobart and Melrose. It read:

P.M. Parker:

For the trouble you have caused, Marjorie Parker will be the next victim. Nothing can stop the Fox and they who try will know the penalty. If you warn anyone of this second success, it will mean you next.

Try and get me. I am the Fox. You will never know the rest of my success. You will miss her at 12 o'clock.

The Fox

Security at the Parker home was doubled, but even a glance at the handwriting by detectives assured them that this latest message was a hoax. Coverage of the manhunt in the *Los Angeles Times* included front-page announcements of increased rewards for the "monster's capture," plus an editorial that was headlined "This Fiend Must Not Escape":

Staggering to the imagination, abhorrent to every human instinct, are the incredibly horrible circumstances surrounding the murder and mutilation of twelve-year-old Marion Parker, lured from her schoolroom last Thursday, subjected by her kidnapper to unknown and unnamable horrors, slain, dismembered and – as a crowning, frightful touch to the hell-born scheme of a fiend incarnate – the pitiful fragments of her hacked-up body wrought into the ghastly guise of a living child and delivered to her father in return for $1,500 "ransom."

The police are doing everything possible to apprehend this fiendish slayer, but this is not a job for the police alone. Every citizen of Los Angeles, every resident of the Southwest, must assist. If every pair of eyes within the area of the murderer's possible movements is vigilantly alert for a man of his description, for his car, and for the numbers of the bills paid him for the little girl's shattered corpse, his chances to elude the gallows will be scant indeed.

The editorial – with its lengthy, dramatic, and overwrought sentences -- was followed by a description of a clean-shaven man with wavy brown hair, believed to be 25 or 30 years of age. Serial numbers of the $20 gold certificates, ranging from K68016901 to K68016975, were also noted, for the benefit of anyone who might be in a position to do business with the fugitive in a filling station, hotel, or restaurant.

On Monday, a coroner's jury convened to examine Marion's case. Dr. Wagner, the first of three witnesses, caused an uproar in the hearing room when he told the panel that he was unable to determine the child's specific time of death – in other words, "I cannot say whether she was killed before her body was so horribly mutilated." There was no evidence of chloroform or any other anesthetic being used, which left the panel to only imagine what kind of horror that Marion experienced.

Mary Holt, from Marion's school, testified next. She gave a description of the kidnapper: "He seemed very well educated and was very courteous and calm. He completely convinced me, and I am always very careful about excusing children, even questioning parents as to identity and reason for the desired absence. I shouldn't have let her go if I had questioned him in the least."

Detective W.W. Warren was the last to take the stand. He recapped the events since Thursday for the coroner's jury and the panel wasted no time in returning its judgment that "Deceased came to her death at the hands of a person or persons unknown to the jury, acting with homicidal intent."

America was a less litigious country in the 1920s than it is today, but Los Angeles school board officials wasted no time in make sure they were covered for the blunder of releasing Marion from school and into the hands of a kidnapper. Mary Holt was still on the witness stand when Superintendent Susan Dorsey issued a statement to the press:

Mrs. Holt had no authority to excuse any child from school. That is done by our vice principal, and then only at the request of the child's parents or guardian. But in this case, there appeared to be an emergency when the man rushed in and claimed there had been an accident and the child's father was calling for her.

I talked to Mrs. Holt and am satisfied that I would have acted as she did if I were confronted with the same circumstances. At that time the vice principal, who is the person in authority entitled to excuse a child from class, was busy with the Christmas program and could not be reached in the few minutes that elapsed.

The fact that nothing has ever befallen our school in the past is evidence that they are as safeguarded as humanly possible.

This assurance from school officials was meant to calm the nerves of the thousands of parents whose children were still in school, but did little to comfort the Parkers. If parents were not reassured, the *Times* also announced that 50 supervisors of attendance and child welfare from the city school system were being mobilized to join the search for Marion's killer.

Of course, some might say – too little, too late.

A private funeral was held for Marion on Monday afternoon at Forest Lawn Cemetery's Little Church of Flowers in Glendale. Dr. Herbert Booth Smith, pastor of Immanuel Presbyterian Church, was in charge of the service. The *Los Angeles Times* described the chapel as "a perfect bower of flowers and potted plants." After the closed-casket service ended at 5:00 p.m., Marion's remains were cremated.

And the search for her killer continued.

Three more suspects were in custody by Monday afternoon. Earl Smith, 23, identified as a "manufacturing dentist," had been jailed on Saturday for grand larceny, and the police also interrogated him about the kidnapping. However, their reasons for doing so have been lost over time. A second prisoner, Gaylord Barnaman, was arrested at a downtown hotel after he identified himself as the "Fox." He demanded radio time to make a statement. The police soon dismissed him as a "psychopathic case."

The third – and most promising – suspect was a telephone operator named Lillian Padley, 22. She was arrested before dawn on Monday morning after neighbors complained of a loud disturbance at her rented quarters near the corner of Fifth Street and Manhattan Place. Officers surrounded the house and Padley ran outside, reportedly screaming, "I didn't kill her! I didn't kill her! They did!" An unnamed man was found sleeping in the house, but after offering a solid alibi, he was released. Lillian was taken downtown to pay a $10 fine for being drunk and disorderly. A search of the house turned up a "grotesque picture of Judas Iscariot," a biblical figure mentioned by name in one letter that was sent to Perry Parker by the "Fox." The cops also found "sharp heel prints on the carpet, etched in blood, a man's undergarment splotched with blood, and several washed towels which appeared once to have been bloodstained." It all seemed very sinister, but in the end, it came to nothing. As the *Times* reported, "While it is doubted whether this house had any connection with the butchery of Marion's body, the young woman is to be detained until further developments."

The police also searched a second house in Los Angeles, after neighbors reported that two men and a woman had moved out "several days ago." A torn and crumped piece of paper was found on the floor with the name "Marion" written on it. Oddly, the *Times* reported that "Although the scrap of paper is of no particular significance, the investigators said, it is believed it is a portion of a draft of one of the ransom notes." Detectives didn't explain how such a clue – if that was really what it was -- could be insignificant, but their search of the house yielded no helpful evidence.

The police were working around the clock. They were spread thin, attempting to search everywhere at once. Near Saugus, two deputies rousted a suspect "resembling" the kidnapper from a northbound Southern Pacific freight train. They chased him into the foothills, firing at him with shotguns, but he managed to give them the slip. He later eluded a larger group of lawmen and about 250 volunteers from the nearby Barker Ranch. Police in Santa Monica were stopping cars at random, looking for any driver who might fit the killer's description after one nervous resident phoned in a possible license number. The L.A. County sheriff's office broadcast an alert for a recent San Quentin parolee – convicted of raping his own daughter – but the suspect's name and description were accidentally omitted from the press reports.

It was a free-for-all. Reward money kept pouring in, leading to more useless leads, crack calls, and crackpots. J. Bruce Goddard, president of the Co-Operative Apartment and Hotel Owners Association of Southern California, appealed to all landlords to aid in the search for the killer by scrutinizing their tenants and searching their apartments if possible.

But in the middle of all the madness, detectives were making progress. A nationwide broadcast description of the roadster that had been used in the kidnapping put detectives in touch with its owner, a doctor in Kansas City, and his description of the thief matched that of Marion's killer. Fingerprints inside of the car got a hit – they belonged to William Edward Hickman, 19, who had been arrested the previous June. He was also a suspect in a robbery back in November.

But that wasn't all.

One of the bloodstained towels that were discovered at the crime scene – stuffed in the cheap, imitation leather suitcase – was marked with the name "Bellevue Arms Apartments," which were located at 1170 Bellevue Avenue. Detectives hurried to the apartment building and began questioning the residents. One of the tenants – who had registered under a false name – was William Hickman. The previous Saturday night, he was seen carrying a suitcase and several bundles to an automobile parked near the building's rear entrance.

Hickman later claimed that he actually talked with police officers at the apartment building and managed to slip past them and disappear, but this seems unlikely. By the time that detectives discovered the link between the building where he lived and the crime scene, Hickman had already skipped town. By the time that he checked out of the Herald Hotel on Tuesday morning, he was already a hunted man.

The self-proclaimed "Fox" and "mastermind" had failed to wipe the fingerprints from the car used to commit his crime before he abandoned it on Saturday night. The fingerprints connected him to other recent offenses, including a November 27 robbery at Jackson's Pharmacy on Sunset Boulevard. The owner, K.D. Jackson, identified his photograph as the robber who came into the store looking for chloroform and ether. He had forced Jackson to lie on the floor while he ransacked the pharmacy. Failing to find ether, he took $80 and some sleeping pills. Hickman was also identified by two other pharmacists who were also robbed. On December 5, he took chloroform, ether, and $156 from the two stores. It was recalled that Hickman was driving the stolen car at the time.

On Monday, the police returned to the Bellevue Arms Apartments and searched apartment 315, where Hickman had been living. In his haste to leave, he had left his breakfast on the table, complete with fingerprints on a milk bottle and a sugar bowl. The prints matched those in the car, and on his booking card from an arrest the previous June.

The Bellevue Arms Apartments, where Hickman lived at the time of the kidnapping. Marion was murdered and dismembered in apartment 315

Amid the clutter of the place – golf balls and clubs, a portable phonograph, scattered clothing, and partially burned letters – detectives found the broken shells of some Brazil nuts, and matched them to fragments that were retrieved from the pockets of Marion's dress.

An arrest warrant was issued for William Edward Hickman on Monday evening and he was formally charged with kidnapping and murder by the Los Angeles district attorney's office on Tuesday, December 20. Municipal Judge Baird signed a bench warrant for his arrest, to facilitate extradition if Hickman was captured outside of California.

Once the charges became public, reporters dug into Hickman's past and found the information about this arrest in June 1927. He had been charged with forgery – while employed at the bank where Perry Parker worked as the personnel officer. Reporters now had a link between the Parkers and the man who committed the horrific crime.

Perry Parker was stunned, but not completely surprised, when he learned of the killer's identity. He told the press, "I recall the unusual manner in which Hickman talked with me about his discharge for forgery. I remember how he asked me for his position again after being granted probation – a probation I protested – and his replies to questions, and the calm manner and voice I heard over the telephone, and lastly the coolness and nerve displayed Saturday night when we met for the exchange, and I am convinced that Hickman was at the other end of the telephone and he took the $1,500."

As for motive, Parker said, "I cannot call to mind any words of madness or revenge that passed while I was talking with Hickman, but I do remember that his reactions to the forgery charges did not seem to be usual. He evinced no nervousness and showed very little concern over the seriousness of his actions. This impressed me very much at the time, but no thought of his planning to harm me or members of my family in return for his discharge entered my mind."

Of course, in June 1927, Perry Parker had no way of knowing that William Hickman had already killed at least one person, and perhaps several more. The banker had believed that he was simply dealing with a troubled young man. He had no idea how troubled Hickman really was.

After Hickman's arrest in June, he entered a guilty charge for forgery, but because he lied about his age, the case was heard in juvenile court.

Hickman was placed on probation – which Perry Parker had argued against – and placed in his mother's custody.

The two of them had gone back to Kansas City, where they had been living before Hickman left home. A few months later, the news that Hickman was wanted for murder stunned his mother and his Kansas City acquaintances. It was there where Hickman had stolen what was now being called the "death car."

When she learned of her son's arrest warrant being issued, Eva Hickman commented to reporters, "It's a terrible mistake. This crime is the work of a fiend. My boy is a good clean boy. I'll never believe it until I hear it from his own lips."

William Edward Hickman – the depraved murdered who was described by his mother as a "good clean boy."

Eva said that her son left Kansas City a few months before to "make his way in the world alone." She had last heard from him in October. He was working as an usher in a Chicago theater and she thought he was still there. He was a "good home boy," she said. He attended church regularly and was a leader in Sunday School activities.

Officials at Central High School in Kansas City, where Hickman had attended, were also shocked to learn of the charges against him. Principal Otto F. Dubach said he had been an exceptional student, "mild-mannered" and "popular." He got good grades and was elected to the student council three years in a row. He served as the vice president of his senior class in 1926. He was also president of the school's chapter of the National Honor Society, president of the Central Webster Club, president of the Central

Classics Club, a member of the debate team, business manager of the school paper, literary editor of the school year book and was voted by his peers as the school's "best boy orator."

William Edward Hickman, who liked to be called "Ed," was a puzzle. Was he the perfect son and student or a cold-blooded killer? Or both?

Once Hickman was identified as Marion's killer, sightings came in from all over the city, throughout California, and beyond. Volunteers were still combing the hills around Saugus, looking for the train jumper who had dodged them on Monday, and the Kern County sheriff had posted men along the Ridge Route from L.A. to prevent Hickman from escaping north to Bakersfield. At 1:00 a.m. on Tuesday morning, a young man fitting Hickman's description used a pay phone in a drugstore at Forty-Eighth and Arlington, in Los Angeles. The pharmacist overheard him telling someone on the other end of the line, "Lay low, for god's sake, lay low!" Four hours later, and a few blocks away, in downtown L.A., a filling station attendant named John Ward claimed that he filled Hickman's gas tank and the fugitive had fled without paying his bill.

In San Luis Obispo, a man who "looked like Hickman" was reportedly seen driving through town, accompanied by a middle-aged passenger. L.A. traffic officers pursued a suspect in a blue Cadillac, losing him downtown before he ditched the car in San Bernardino, stole another car and drove to Redlands, where he crashed the second auto and fled on foot, successfully eluding his pursuers. Howard Mitchell, an attorney and officer of the Automobile Club of Southern California, said that he spotted Hickman outside of Pomona. He was riding a motorcycle and wearing a heavy sweater and tall boots, as if "prepared for rough country."

Homer Mays, an African-American barber in Monrovia, said that a rare white customer came into his shop on Monday evening and ordered a shave and heavy hair dressing to flatten his wavy hair. The barber commented that the customer looked like Hickman and added, "there's a high price on his head." The customer frowned at the comment, Maus said, and added, "You don't know how close you are getting to it."

By that time, 12,000 members of the American Legion had mobilized in Southern California and were prepared to join in the search. Soon, Hickman fever had spread nationwide. Hickman was everywhere – and nowhere – all at the same time.

San Francisco police – where Hickman actually was – were on alert Monday night after a man named Leslie Russell reported a strange encounter in the Mission District. Russell was in his car with the engine running when a man fitting Hickman's description approached him and said that he had come from Los Angeles and needed to "lie low until the excitement died down." Russell sped off to find a patrolman but the Hickman look-alike was gone when he came back with officers. Meanwhile, patrons at the local post office reported Hickman – or someone who looked just like him – mailing off a package to Kansas City.

Farther north, at Yreka, not far from the Oregon state line, a waitress swore that she had served the fugitive on Monday night. She said that he was extremely nervous, once dropping his coffee cup from his shaking hand. In the other direction, to the south, California authorities urged Mexican police to keep an eye out for the kidnapper, who they were sure was heading south of the border. Baja California Governor Abelardo Rodriguez deputized a special force of volunteers to patrol 150 miles of border around the clock, scouring the desert for Hickman. Elsewhere, police were on alert from Denver to Portland, Oregon, to Kansas City, and to Hartford, Arkansas, where Hickman had been born.

Despite thousands of watchful eyes, there was no sign of him anywhere.

After checking out of his hotel, Hickman went north, bound for Seattle. He knew that the police would be looking for a young man traveling alone, so he began looking for company. He found his first passenger thumbing rides outside of Davis, east of Sacramento, and drove the man as far as Redding, where they separated after having supper in a coffee shop. The other patrons were talking about the reward being offered for Marion Parker's killer, but never glanced in Hickman's direction. The young man was made nervous by the conversation, though, and rushed through his meal, anxious to be on his way.

About 20 miles further north, he spotted two more hitchhikers around 8:00 p.m. James Nelson and Irwin Mowrey were on their way to Portland to spend the holidays with relatives, and Hickman told them that he could take them all the way. The men noticed that Hickman kept a .45 automatic close at hand – either on the seat next to him or tucked into a pocket on the driver's door – and asked him about it. Hickman said that he carried it for protection, worried that he might be stopped and robbed somewhere. The hitchhikers were only vaguely aware of the manhunt in Los Angeles and had not paid attention to the description of the fugitive. They had no idea that they were riding with the state's most wanted criminal.

It was near 10:00 p.m. when they approached the Oregon state line. Near the small town of Hilt, California, Hickman began looking for a place to pull off the highway. When Nelson and Mowrey asked what he was doing when he turned off onto a dirt logging road, he explained that he'd heard the police were stopping people at the state line, and he didn't want to take a chance because he had two gallons of illegal whiskey in the trunk. They would rest until midnight, when he thought the lawmen might relax their vigil.

Two hours later, they started north again, with Nelson driving. Mowrey was in the passenger seat and Hickman was stretched out in the back, pretending to sleep as they approached the state line. He had been wrong about the roadblocks being taken down at midnight. They were stopped and officers peered into the car. They were looking for a single young man, however, not three fellows traveling together. They waved the Hudson through the checkpoint and Hickman relaxed as the miles passed.

It was just after noon on Wednesday when they arrived in Portland. Hickman dropped off his passengers downtown at the Imperial Hotel. He got out to stretch his legs and was embarrassed when his pistol clattered to the pavement. He snatched it up, got into the car, and drove off without a word, leaving Nelson and Mowrey standing on the sidewalk. It was midafternoon before one of the hitchhikers saw a newspaper with Hickman's face on the front page and called the police. A description was broadcast of the stolen Hudson and its California license number and officers all over the region went on alert.

But it was too late. Hickman was gone. He had already crossed into Washington.

Even though it looked as though Hickman was far away from Los Angeles, the LAPD continued to behave as if their quarry was close to home. This mindset was encouraged by callers like C.F. Kaufman, from Pomona, who had once worked with the fugitive at the same bank where Perry Parker worked and claimed that Hickman had stopped by his house to ask for directions to Tijuana, Mexico. Dorothy Taylor, a teenage waitress who was in jail for writing bad checks, told police that Hickman resembled her best friend's "sweetie." Yet another lead, from realtor William Ryan, claimed that Hickman and a companion were house-hunting in Chico.

Wholesale arrests of young, dark-haired men continued in Los Angeles, even after Police Chief Herman Cline heard from Portland police that Hickman had been sighted in Oregon, heading north. The *Times* reported "dozens" of arrests, some accompanied by threats of mob violence, as would-be vigilantes tried to even the score for Marion's murder.

A Hickman look-alike named Richard Pleaux was arrested in Tucson and displayed an LAPD "parole card" to detectives there. Even though Chief Cline denied that they existed, his men actually had hastily printed "exemption certificates" for suspects who looked like Hickman but had already been questioned and cleared. No "get out of jail free card" helped Michael O'Neill, though – by Wednesday afternoon the dark-haired young man had been arrested no less than five times by different police officers.

The real Hickman made it to Seattle at 6:00 p.m. on Wednesday night and his first stop was a movie theater. He used one of the $20 gold certificates from the ransom money to buy his ticket, pocketing the change. It was a foolish risk, but perhaps he believed that he was far enough away from L.A. that it didn't matter.

But some have suggested that perhaps he wanted to get caught for his crime. This idea is based on a letter that was mailed to Seattle's Police Chief William Searing on Wednesday night. The letter was almost rejected for insufficient postage – the sender had used a single, one-cent stamp – before a clerk made note of the addressee and the word "Fox" that was written in one corner of the envelope. The letter read:

> *I am tired of this. Will I be given fair play if I surrender? I did not intend to kill Marion. I did not mean to harm her. I only wanted to put her to sleep. I did not want her to suffer, as she was a good girl. She was not afraid of me at any time and did not suffer. She only wanted to go home and would have left in safety if my plans had not failed. Will this make any difference?*
> *This is the truth.*
>
> *The Fox*

Even though Hickman would later deny having written the letter, it certainly *sounded* like him. But if he did write it, he apparently had second thoughts and did not wait around for a reply. Leaving the theater around 8:30 p.m., he watched a squad car pass and assumed the police were hunting him. He didn't know it, but the letter to Chief Searing had not been delivered yet, and no one from the theater ever acknowledged receiving one of the ransom bills.

Chilled by the Seattle weather, he went in search of a men's clothing store, where he could buy a warmer outfit. It was nearly 9:00 p.m. before he found one that was still open. He selected a hat, gloves, and some thermal underwear. The bill came to $5 and, instead of using the change from the movie theater, he produced #69 of the 75 gold certificates that Perry Parker had given to his daughter's kidnapper.

As Hickman walked back to his car, his paranoia kicked into high gear. He was sure that the sales clerk had recognized him. He spotted a newsboy walking behind him and imagined that he was in pursuit. He hurried to the Hudson and drove off as quickly as traffic would allow. Whatever thoughts that he may have had about surrendering in Seattle left his mind and he began to focus only on evading the police.

By that night, the Seattle police had gone into action and began setting up roadblocks around the city, cutting off every avenue of escape. But it was too late. Hickman was already gone.

Hickman slipped out of Seattle and doubled back toward Oregon. He believed that the manhunt would be concentrated to the north. The police had tracked him this far, he thought, so they must think that he was heading to Canada. He would outfox them by going backwards. However, in Kent, Washington, the "mastermind" used another ransom bill, which the police used to map his escape route.

About 60 miles south of Olympia, he stopped just long enough to steal a set of local plates from an unattended Ford. He made it through Oregon without being stopped, and by daylight on Thursday, he drove through Pendleton for the second time in as many days, turning to the east, and following the Columbia River. He reverted back to his idea about "safety in numbers" and picked up two hitchhikers, Bill and Jack Merrill, for company.

The Merrill brothers were on their way home to Garfield, Washington, for Christmas, after months of farm work in Oregon. Since Hickman was going east, he offered them a ride as far as Pendleton. The brothers rode in back and Hickman told them that he was going home for the holidays, too. In his case, to Salt Lake City, which was a break from his college studies in Olympia, Washington. At one point, unable to help himself, he pulled out the .45 automatic with a flourish and showed it off. He carried the gun for protection, he explained, because he traveled with a lot of money. He let the boys handle the gun, and if they'd had any idea he was Hickman, they could have captured him without any trouble. When they left the car, they assumed they had been riding with a bootlegger. They wouldn't find out about his fugitive status until later.

Hickman was finally caught thanks to some quick thinking on the part of a Los Angeles newsman and an old-fashioned Oregon lawman.

Early on Thursday morning, Walter Clausen, the L.A. bureau chief for the Associated Press and a part-time captain in the U.S. Army Reserve's military intelligence department, came up with an idea. He didn't know where Hickman was exactly, but he had been up most of the night, collating reports from Washington and Oregon, plotting the strange, erratic progress of Hickman's Hudson sedan. Now it was snowing in northern Washington, which meant the roads and passes into Canada would be closed. Clausen believed that Hickman might double back instead of waiting out the storm. And he was right, although snow had nothing to do with Hickman's decision.

Excited at the prospect of participating in the manhunt, even at a distance, Clausen wired all Associated Press subscribers in the Pacific Northwest an urgent description of the stolen car, complete with the license plates – which Hickman had replaced – and the engine serial numbers.

Near lunchtime, Pendleton Police Chief Tom Gurdane received an anxious telephone call from Parker Branin, the editor at the local *East Oregonian* newspaper. There was something on the wire that he needed to see.

Gurdane walked over to the newspaper office. The big, rugged man was the kind of old-fashioned peace officer that had been assigned to the old Oregon Trail for decades. He spoke quietly, put up with no nonsense, and kept busy, even in a relatively quiet town like Pendleton. He was just about to make the biggest arrest in his career.

On the way, Gurdane met Buck Lieuallen of the state highway patrol and asked him to tag along. The newspaper editor met them in the lobby and began talking fast. Hickman had been spotted. He had used a ransom bill to pay for gas in Arlington, just 60 miles west of Pendleton, and was heading east toward Pendleton on a state highway that paralleled the Umatilla River.

With Lieuallen driving, the two lawmen left in the state patrol car since Gurdane had no official jurisdiction outside of Pendleton. They drove about 20 miles to Echo and then Lieuallen parked his cruiser on the dirt shoulder of the road, positioned so that they could see the next curve ahead. They didn't have to wait long before the green Hudson came into view. The driver had dark hair and was wearing sunglasses, even though the day was overcast and gray.

Gurdane was convinced it was William Hickman.

The Hudson sped past them and the lawmen followed in pursuit. When the other car picked up speed, Lieuallen reached over and turned on the siren. The pursuit – which reporters later referred to as a "breakneck chase" – lasted about two minutes. Hickman pulled over about a mile and a half down the road. Gurdane and Lieuallen jumped out and approached the car with guns drawn. Gurdane was on the driver's side and Lieuallen walked up on the right, covering the two passengers in the back seat.

Hickman rolled down his window and smiled at Gurdane. "Was I speeding?" he asked.

Gurdane ignored him. "What's your name?"

Hickman never missed a beat. He knew the name of the car's owner and offered it. "My name is Peck," he replied.

"Where are you from?"

Hickman quickly answered. "Seattle. I've been attending college over there and I'm going to visit my mother."

Gurdane later told reporters, "I covered him with my gun and opened the door with my left hand and told him to get out. When he started to get out, a .45 automatic dropped to the running board." When Gurdane asked him what he was doing with the gun, Hickman said that it was customary to carry one when traveling.

"You don't need to keep it between your knees," Gurdane snapped.

Hickman was placed into custody and searched by the lawmen. A glance down past the steering wheel revealed a sawed-off shotgun, lying on the floorboard.

Lieuallen searched him and pulled one of the crumpled $20 gold certificates from Hickman's pockets. Lieuallen then searched the car, which contained another $1,400 in bills. Hickman glanced at the bills in the policeman's hands and then shrugged to the officers. "Well," he said, "I guess it's all over."

As the handcuffs were snapped over Hickman's wrists, he let out a hysterical bray of laughter.

"THE FOX" REVEALED

William Edward Hickman was born February 1, 1908, in Hartford, Arkansas. Because he had the same first name as his father, Hickman was always referred to as either "Edward," or, more commonly, "Ed."

When he was 12, his parents, William and Eva, separated, and his mother moved him, his three older brothers, and younger sister, to Kansas City, Missouri. Ed had no trouble fitting in at Central High School. He was both popular and successful, serving as the vice president of his senior class, president of three honor societies, editor of the school yearbook, business manager of the school newspaper, and a member of both the debating team and the student council. He even received an award as the school's best orator. Beneath his 1926 graduating picture, there is mention of his excellent scholastic standing, record of extracurricular activities, and the high standards that he set, which were unequaled in the history of the school. According to his mother, Hickman was also a member of the First Baptist Church of Kansas City and played on the Sunday School's basketball team.

When the police had contacted Eva Hickman about her son's involvement in the Parker case, she had become distraught. This was no mere concern, or worry, about her son. Those who knew her had long described her as deeply disturbed. While she was pregnant with Ed, her fourth child, she suffered from a series of emotional disturbances, allegedly brought on by her husband's affairs with other women. Ed was born prematurely – some doctors later suggested because Eva's emotional problems affected her baby – and was initially thought to be stillborn. Doctors revived him and after a few months, he was developing in a normal, healthy manner.

During his early childhood, Eva spent most of her time in a fragile state. When pregnant with Ed's sister, Mary, two years younger than Ed, Eva lapsed into spells when she threatened to harm her children. She also threatened suicide and once attempted to poison herself. When Ed was three-years-old, his mother spent a year in the State Lunatic Asylum in Little Rock.

Then, in the spring of 1921, Eva left her husband and took the children to Kansas City. Ed thrived in high school. He enjoyed success in all his activities, and for those years, Hickman was happy. His life was going in a positive direction and his friendly, relaxed personality won him a lot of friends. He was popular, outgoing, and good at everything he tried.

After being given an award for his oratory skills, he set out to win a national competition. He worked hard, putting a tremendous amount of pressure on himself, and spent an entire year preparing for the contest. In the finals, though, he choked and ended up with only a $5 consolation prize. His hopes were completely crushed. Everyone assumed the carefree boy would get over his loss and move on to the next big thing, but he didn't. Ed Hickman began to change – and it was not a change for the better.

Ed stopped spending time with his friends, avoiding them at school, and staying home so that he didn't have to make excuses for failing to spend time with them. He worked a few odd jobs, but could never get enthused about anything he was doing. Hickman had always been successful at everything he tried, but when he worked hard at something he believed he was very good at, and failed, his reaction was far more emotional than anyone around him would have expected. He stopped working hard at his studies, and while he joined a few clubs during his senior year, he eventually quit them one after another. His friends abandoned him and his academic level plummeted.

The only person that Hickman seemed to show interest in was his childhood friend, Vincent Doran, who lived across the street. Doran suffered from tuberculosis and Hickman visited him every day. Vincent was allowed few visitors, but Hickman was always welcome. When the young man died in February 1926, Ed was one of the pallbearers at his funeral.

Hickman's state of mind grew worse after that. People who once knew him told journalists that he was a good, kind boy who took his failures a bit too seriously. It was difficult for them to believe that he was capable of something as horrific as murdering a young girl. Those who knew him as a child in Arkansas felt generally the same.

But there was another side to Hickman that would only be revealed as the investigation into his history continued.

After working odd jobs during the summer after his graduation, Hickman enrolled in the Kansas City Junior College. He attended classes for just nine days and then never returned. He worked at a few other jobs, including at a public library, and then at the Kiger Jewelry Company after receiving a recommendation from J.L. Laughlin, the vice principal at Central High School.

While working at the library, Hickman became friendly with a man named Welby Hunt. Edward quit his job at Kiger's and in late November, he and Hunt robbed a confectionary. They got away with $70. Realizing that he had a knack for crime, Hickman got restless. With a gun, car, and money, he convinced Hunt that they should go to California. They left in December 1926, and Hickman told his mother that he was going to try and get into the movie business.

Hickman and Hunt were in Los Angeles on Christmas Eve when they committed their next robbery. They entered a pharmacy owned by Ivy Thoms and he was there that night, along with his wife, and three customers. Wearing masks and with pistols in hand, the two robbers were surprised by the appearance of Officer D.J. Oliver, who was walking his police beat that night and happened to stop in to visit his friends, Mr. and Mrs. Thoms. Oliver started to raise his hands, pretending to surrender, but pulled his weapon instead. A gun battle followed, with the inexperienced Hickman and Hunt firing wildly as they tried to escape from the store. Officer Oliver was wounded in the abdomen, but survived. Ivy Thoms was shot in the chest and died on the spot.

Hickman and Hunt escaped the pharmacy, but left with no cash. Looking for work, Hickman got a job in January 1927 as a page for the First National Trust and Savings Bank, where Perry Parker was employed. Parker's job was such that he likely would have never become well acquainted with Hickman – until Ed was caught forging checks. After being put on probation, Hickman returned to Kansas City and spent six weeks in the fall of 1927 working as an usher at a movie theater. It was as close to the "Hollywood movie business" that he would ever get. He was eventually fired after the manager discovered that he was spending most of his time sneaking in to watch the movies.

In Kansas City, Hickman resumed his criminal activities. In October, he stole a car belonging to a traveling salesman and drove it all the way to Chicago. On October 11, 1927, a man whose description matched Hickman strangled a young girl in Milwaukee, Wisconsin. When Hickman's picture was published in newspapers throughout the country as the man suspected of killing Marion Parker, the police in Milwaukee requested that once he was captured, Hickman be interrogated for the murder in their city, too.

Hickman went to Michigan, then Pennsylvania. In Chester, Pennsylvania, on October 29, 1927, a gas station manager named James Claire was shot and killed during a robbery by a man whose description sounded an awful lot like Hickman's. Just as with the murder in Milwaukee, Pennsylvania authorities recognized Hickman's photo once it was plastered across every newspaper in the county. They, too, asked that he be questioned about the Clare murder.

Unbelievably, in addition to committing crimes, Hickman did some sightseeing while on his trip. He drove to Gettysburg and took a tour of the battlefield. He drove through Maryland and to Washington, D.C. and spent a short time in New York, before seeing West Virginia and Ohio. It was in Ohio that he successfully robbed three stores in a mere half-hour time frame. By the time that he returned to Kansas City with his stolen automobile, he had driven more than 4,000 miles and had committed several more petty robberies.

The high school scholar, athlete, and "good boy" had become an experienced criminal.

On November 7, 1927, Hickman stole the infamous Chrysler roadster from Dr. Herbert Mentz. Just 11 days later, he was back in California, where he robbed a pharmacy of $30. It was then that he settled into the apartment at the Bellevue Arms and tried to decide what he wanted to do next.

On Thanksgiving Day – November 23, 1927 – Hickman was taking a drive down to San Diego when he met a couple that needed a lift to Los Angeles. Hickman picked them up, and the three became friendly. They were so friendly, in fact, that the man and Hickman made plans to meet three days later and knock over a few stores for some cash. They robbed a pharmacy on November 27, and two more pharmacies on December 5. Along with the money, Hickman took sleeping tablets and chloroform. When his accomplice asked why he needed these things, Hickman explained that he had an idea about committing a bigger crime that would earn him some real money.

He wanted to kidnap a child for ransom, he said. That was where the real money was.

PAYING THE PRICE FOR MURDER

After his arrest on the Oregon highway, Hickman was taken into custody and brought to the Pendleton city jail. A crowd gathered as news of his capture spread through town. The people of Pendleton were curious about the young man they had been reading about in the papers. There was no angry mob, or vigilantes looking for justice. The Pendleton folks just wanted to see what all the fuss was about.

But the same could not be said for those in Los Angeles. The night before, a robbery suspect named Ralph McCoy was caught after a downtown chase. An onlooker called out that McCoy was "that child murderer William Edward Hickman," even though McCoy looked nothing like the kidnapper and killer of Marion Parker. McCoy was taken to the city jail and placed in a cell with other prisoners. He was strangled to death at some point in the night. Each of the prisoners was questioned, but all insisted that McCoy had killed himself with his own necktie.

Chief Herman Cline sent word to Oregon, asking that extra guards be posted around Hickman. He spoke to reporters that day, "Thank God, they've got him," he said. "I was afraid Hickman would be killed on sight and then we would never learn the details of this horrible tragedy." District Attorney Keyes added, "We know that we have the arch criminal in California murder history. We are devoted to speeding this case to trial."

The Parker house had been under guard for days, watched over by three plainclothes detectives inside and outside the house. A policeman arrived at the Parker home and reported Hickman's to capture a guard outside. He then went inside and quietly told Perry Parker. Parker then took Geraldine into another room to give her the news. She had been under constant treatment since Marion's murder. Neither she, nor Marjorie, were ever told the specific details of the crime.

Parker made a statement to the press: "I am certainly thankful. I am thankful not only for myself, but for the parents of all other children that such a dangerous man has been apprehended. This thing is too terrible to talk about adequate punishment for the man. This strain has been terrible on all of us; I am reassured and only hope there has been no mistake." Parker added that he was comfortable allowing the law to handle the situation. He believed completely, he said, in the American system of justice.

As soon as news reached Los Angeles of Hickman's arrest in Oregon, a grand jury was convened for a special session at 7:30 p.m. It quickly returned an indictment for kidnapping and murder. A warrant was issued, and Hickman was ordered held without bail. Extradition papers were being rushed through the system.

Chief of Detectives George Contreras flew to Oregon the next morning. He took along Detectives H.G. Taylor and E.M. Harman to help get the prisoner back to Los Angeles. Detective Cline stated that extradition papers would be picked up by officers in Sacramento, where Governor Young promised to have them by the time police arrived. Cline assigned an extra guard to bring Hickman back to prevent Hickman from being "lynched by an angry mob of citizens."

Newspaper reports stated that Hickman was completely at ease when he was brought into the police station and was overheard telling Officer Lieuallen, "This is going to be interesting before it is all over."

After the indictment, Hickman was told that he had been named as the murderer of Marion Parker. His first impulse was to laugh out loud, startling everyone in the room.

Reporters got their chance to ask questions, but Hickman refused to answer most of them. However, he did query, "Do they only kill by hanging in California?" Before anyone could reply, he answered the question himself – "Oh, this is not California, is it?

When asked to pose for a photograph, flanked by the two lawmen that brought him in, he asked, "What should I look like? A crook?"

For reasons unknown, Hickman didn't spill his story to the police, but rather to Parker Branin, city editor of the *East Oregonian*, and John Beckwith, a court reporter.

In a rambling tale that often made little sense, Hickman admitted that he had rented the apartment at the Bellevue Arms and related how he had

Hickman in custody in Oregon. Pendleton Police Chief Tom Gurdane is on the left and Hickman is flanked on the right by state patrol Officer Buck Lieuallen.

gone to San Diego on Thanksgiving Day. He had picked up a couple, whom he identified as Andrew Cramer and a woman he called June Dunning. Hickman told them that he made his living doing holdups and felt that if he could get acquainted with an older accomplice, they could work with less risk. They began holding up drugstores but Hickman claimed that his intention was not to become a crook – he wanted to raise enough money to go back to college in Kansas City. He also claimed that the kidnapping of Marion Parker had not been his idea. Cramer had suggested kidnapping a child and Hickman remembered Perry Parker at the bank that he'd been fired from.

"I happened to remember that Mr. Parker had a daughter," he said. "I was there in the bank several days, and I noticed especially, I remembered that it was his daughter and he would take her downtown and buy her lunch and she was around the bank like she was a big man."

Hickman was sure that he could get Parker to give up the $1,500 he needed to get back to Kansas City and enroll in college.

Hickman said that he and Cramer had watched the Parker house and once had seen Marion riding her bicycle alone. On Thursday morning, he had parked by the house early and watched Marion and Marjorie leave for school. He admitted trying to get their attention as they rode the streetcar, just as Marjorie later told the police. It was then that Hickman decided to pick Marion up at school. He also admitted that his "plan" was badly executed. He didn't know the girls were twins, he didn't know Marion's name, and it had only worked out because Mary Holt — whose hair had turned white since the kidnapping — had fallen for his ruse.

Unlike Mrs. Holt, Marion immediately began asking questions about her father — what had happened, who had hit him — and Hickman made up answers as he went along.

He told the editor and court reporter that Marion never seemed to think she was in danger. She was more worried about her father's well-being than her own. As they drove, Hickman and Marion talked about movies and comic strips, discussing their favorite characters. Hickman said, "I really kind of liked her. I could not look her in the face when I told her she was kidnapped. When I told her nothing had happened to her father, she didn't worry or scream or anything. She took it as calm as could be."

They drove around all afternoon, Hickman making stops to send telegrams to the Parker home, where Marion's family was waiting nervously. That evening, he took Marion to see a movie at the Rialto Theater in Alhambra. They had laughed a lot and from the way Hickman described it, Marion had a rather pleasant time until things occurred that were out of Hickman's hands.

It was after the movie excursion, Hickman claimed, that Andrew Cramer got involved. Hickman swore that his role in the crime had been to pick up Marion, handle the messages to Mr. Parker, and collect the money. He said that he had turned the girl over to Cramer on Thursday night, after the trip to the movies. He did not see her again until Friday night, when he had her write a letter to her father that made it sound as if she was being treated badly. Hickman said that Marion did not like Cramer and would beg to stay with him instead. But Hickman claimed that he was intimidated by Cramer and so he didn't make any trouble.

He never saw Marion alive again, he said. On Saturday, Cramer showed up at his apartment with her dismembered body in a suitcase. Cramer told the shocked younger man that she had been crying too much, and he decided to stop her permanently. Besides, he added, the police were becoming more and more suspicious and killing Marion would destroy any evidence.

Hickman shook his head as he looked at Branin and Beckwith. "I am terribly sorry that she was killed, because I sure liked her," he said, and then he started to cry.

Hickman said that he had no idea that Cramer planned to kill her. He was heartbroken when he found out, but was terrified of his accomplice and fled the city. With the police hot on his trail, Hickman first went to San Francisco, where he said he planned to meet up with Cramer. But when he got there, his accomplice was nowhere to be found. Frightened and desperate, Hickman began his journey across Oregon, which led to his capture.

Hickman's confession was stunning and was printed in newspapers throughout the country. However, as investigators would soon discover, there was little about the "confession" that was the truth. Hickman loved to brag and talk. As with his inappropriate laughter in dire situations, he just couldn't help himself.

Locked up in the Pendleton jail while he awaited extradition, he bragged wildly to his fellow inmates. At one point, he claimed that he had been stopped by four different LAPD officers while he was making his getaway from Los Angeles.

Rumors circulated for years that this was not an idle claim. Stories claimed that detectives had the chance to grab Hickman while he was at the Bellevue Arms, but delayed their arrest. Since Marion's body was found only hours before – and it was a Sunday – there had not been time for a reward to be posted for the killer's capture. Corrupt detectives had decided to wait to apprehend the killer in hopes of collecting a cash reward. When Hickman escaped, the story was covered up. In truth, though, there is no evidence to say that this ever happened. Most likely, it was just one of the many stories concocted by Hickman while behind bars.

Because there were more – many more. He continued to blame his accomplice for Marion's murder, but couldn't help but enhance his own notoriety. He loved telling the story of using one of the ransom bills at the diner in L.A. on Sunday, just hours after Marion's body had been recovered.

He said that the waitress asked him if he was afraid to be flashing around a wad of $20 bills. No, he bragged, he wasn't afraid. They chatted for a while and when the waitress asked him his name, he simply said, "You'd sure be surprised if you knew."

Hundreds of miles to the south, the Los Angeles legal community was moving as swiftly as possible. District Attorney Asa Keyes had decided to join the parade of lawmen to Oregon and he cited the fear that Oregon residents might lynch Hickman as his reason for travel – not, as some reporters claimed, to get his face on the front page of the newspaper.

By now, the claim that Hickman had an alleged accomplice had reached L.A. Some detectives were not surprised by the news. A few had theorized that another man – and a possible woman – had assisted Hickman in some manner. District Attorney Keyes didn't believe it, though. He told newsmen, "In my opinion, Hickman had no accomplice in this brutal murder. If he did, it will be amazing to me. Until I talk with him and learn more about what he has to say, I cannot give a definite opinion, but it seems to me if he had help, he certainly would have to split the ransom money with his accomplice."

At the same time that news was being made in Los Angeles and Pendleton, Hickman's arrest was wreaking havoc in Kansas City. The EXTRA editions of the local newspapers were in high demand as everyone tried to get the latest news about the local boy gone bad. Eva Hickman, however, was not one of those seeking out the headlines. When she was told of her son's capture and partial confession, she literally collapsed. She sobbed, "It can't be true! If they've caught the slayer of that little girl, it can't be my son."

In El Paso, Texas, reporters tracked down William Thomas Hickman, Eva's former husband and Ed's absent father. He was working in the Southern Pacific Railroad yard as a crane operator. Denying that his son was abnormal in any way, he wept as he spoke about the last time that he had seen his son in Kansas City in October 1926: "I would rather be dead and in hell a thousand times than to think that a child of mine would commit such an atrocious crime. I cannot understand what could have happened to him and to change him into such a fiend as the murder indicates he is, if he really did it."

In the Pendleton jail, Hickman continued to brag and boast – until the wind was knocked out of his sails on Friday, December 23.

In Los Angeles, the police were investigating his claims of an accomplice. Detectives learned that there was not one, but two Andrew Cramers. First, there was an Oliver Andrew Cramer who, like Hickman, went by his middle name. Cramer admitted knowing Ed Hickman, but he had been arrested the previous August and had been in jail ever since. He had a solid alibi – he was locked up at the time of Marion's murder. He did, however, have a brother, whose middle name was also Andrew and he had a girlfriend whose name he thought was June Dunning. Was this the man the police were looking for? Was he the real killer of Marion Parker?

Nope.

Frank Andrew Cramer also knew Hickman, and he had a girlfriend, but her name was Rose, not June. Furthermore, he had been arrested on a different charge right around the time that his brother was arrested. He had also been behind bars since August. It was impossible for him to have been involved in the kidnapping and murder, as Hickman claimed. Cramer made his own statement to the press. "I know him," he said bitterly. "I don't know why he picks on me."

Hickman was visibly shaken when he was told of Cramer's alibi. He continued to stick to his story, but no one believed him at this point.

Chief Herman Cline had initially been willing to entertain the idea of an accomplice, but by the time he learned of Cramer's alibi, he was convinced that Hickman acted alone. He told the press, "The story of Hickman having an accomplice is an absurdity. We previously have checked out every angle of his asserted accomplice and have found the story false and weak. We are after the truth of this matter, and I am convinced we shall find it when Hickman is faced with the facts by those who know the intricate details of the Parker crime."

Hickman's story of an accomplice had failed, so he started looking for a new angle. He quickly found it. Once he realized that his scheme to pin the murder on Andrew Cramer had failed, Hickman recalled the Leopold and Loeb case, in which the plea was guilty by reason of insanity. Rather than face execution, those two "masterminds" were confined to prison for the rest of their lives. A short time later, he told one of the guards, "I wonder if I could pretend I was crazy. How does a fellow act when he's crazy? Do you just have to talk a little off, or do you have to rave around?"

Dr. W.D. McClary of Pendleton, who managed the nearby asylum, had already examined Hickman. He told newspaper reporters:

His mind seems clear. He told a straight, coherent story and was never at a loss for words. There was nothing about him to indicate insanity. He did not differ a bit from hundreds of thousands of other young men. As to whether Hickman is given to sadistic practices I cannot tell. I observed him only casually and did not have the opportunity to make a deep study of him. I saw nothing out of the ordinary about him, nothing that would justify a defense of insanity.

He says that he does not like girls, that he is deeply religious, and his ambition was to become a minister. Several times he made mention of God, and in discussing his capture took that attitude that since God willed it, it had to be.

But Hickman was merely playing the next stage of his game. He was resuming the role of "The Fox" for the Los Angeles detectives who had just arrived in Pendleton.

On Christmas Eve, Oregon Governor I.L. Patterson signed the extradition papers that would return the prisoner to Los Angeles. When District Attorney Keyes told Hickman of his impending return to LA, charged with a death penalty offense, the young man flew into a frenzy, wailing and moaning on the floor of his cell, screaming that he did not kill Marion. His fellow inmates, many of them hardened felons, offered no sympathy. They sneered at his behavior and expressed the sentiment that he'd get what he deserved. It was common among convicts to be disgusted with those who abused or murdered children.

Disgusted by his antics, Chief Gurdane sneered, "The Fox has become a rat."

Harassed by the other prisoners, Hickman hunkered down in his cell. Reality was settling in and he began to genuinely worry about facing the gallows. Around 4:00 p.m., he collapsed onto his bunk and fell into a sleep that was so deep that the prison guards checked him several times to make sure that he was still breathing.

Later that night, knowing that he would be sent back to Los Angeles the next morning, Hickman made two rather foolish suicide attempts. He began with a headfirst dive from his top bunk onto the floor. For that, he got a headache and a bump on his head, but nothing more. Next, he tied a handkerchief around his throat and tried to hang himself from a beam in his cell. Hearing a loud groan, several guards rushed to his cell. He was hanging limp but several minutes later, they had revived him.

Chief Cline was disgusted. "Listen Hickman," he growled, "are you going to be a yellow cur or are you going to brace up and come along on this trip like a man?"

Hickman's only reply was a low, keening moan.

Cline shook his head and ordered his men to take him away.

It was difficult to determine if these were actual attempts at suicide or part of Hickman's plan to escape the noose by pretending to be insane. Most felt these acts were simply part of a series of events designed to build evidence that pointed to insanity. The events were documented and did make the papers, and so, if Hickman was trying to call attention to behavior that could help an insanity defense, his actions were successful.

Of course, there is a certain amount of comic irony to Hickman attempting to commit suicide by strangulation in order to avoid being hanged.

It was just past daylight on December 25 when Chief Cline returned to Hickman's cell. He spoke to him directly in his no-nonsense manner, telling Hickman that the case was getting all kinds of publicity that a movie cameraman was going to get footage of him leaving the jail for newsreels. Cline pointed out that it was up to Hickman as to how he wanted to be presented in the news. He could walk out like a man, or he could break down again and be seen on camera acting like a fool. It must have been a difficult decision for Hickman. He knew that he could use the publicity to look insane in newsreels all over the country. But he decided to walk out like a man. Still plotting and calculating, he appeared cool and collected as he left the Pendleton jail for the bus that would take him to the train station. Hickman was handcuffed to his two guards – Dick Lucas and Harry Raymond. Nobody could shoot Hickman down without also gunning down the two officers. He was safe from whatever crowd might be outside.

When he arrived at the train station, he looked at the 500 or more people who had come down to watch his departure. Their faces were angry and many shouted threats at him. Hickman must have realized that this small crowd was representative of how most of the country now felt about him. They would likely have torn him to pieces if not for the protection offered by the police.

Hickman was loaded aboard a prison car that was attached to a Union Pacific train headed for Portland. From there, he would be transferred to another prison car that was attached to a Los Angeles-bound Southern Pacific train. During the ride, Cline bombarded Hickman with questions. Hickman broke down – again – and told Cline that he had been the one who had murdered and dismembered Marion. There was no one named Andrew Cramer. He had no accomplice – he had acted alone. He told the entire story to Cline, and added that he planned to plead guilty and use an insanity defense. He wanted the judge to be aware of every detail of his story, which he agreed to write in a full and complete statement. Cline encouraged this, of course, assuring Hickman that a judge would be apt to be more lenient if he knew the truth.

Meanwhile, in Los Angeles, detectives continued their search of Hickman's apartment at the Bellevue Arms. They had discovered enough to make them believe that Hickman had killed Marion there.

In Oregon, Tom Gurdane and Buck Lieuallen were basking in the spotlight for their capture of Hickman. When it came to the reward money, though, they tried to be diplomatic. They stated that they did not want money that had been offered by individuals, but saw no reason why they should not take what was offered by Los Angeles banks and other organizations. That was legitimate reward money and they had legitimately earned it. Both men likely spent their Christmas Day figuring out how to spend the money that would soon be coming their way.

Hickman spent his Christmas on the train, but when it arrived in Portland on time at 6:10 p.m., he wasn't on it. En route, detectives on the train received a wire from Portland Chief of Police Jenkins, warning that a mob of more than 2,000 angry citizens were waiting for Hickman at Union Station. Jenkins suggested that Hickman be removed from the train at Montavilla, five miles east of Portland. When the train arrived in Montavilla, a police car rushed the prisoner to the Portland city jail to wait for the Southern Pacific connection to arrive. After a four-hour wait, Hickman boarded a train for Los Angeles.

At the Parker home in Los Angeles, it was the worst Christmas of their lives. They had no plans for the holiday season. The happy spirit that had surrounded the holiday in previous years was gone – likely for good. Marion's murder had brought the family more sorrow than they ever could have imagined. Marjorie would be able to open her gifts, but there was no joy in it since she and Marion had always loved opening their presents together.

"We have no plans for Christmas," Perry Parker told reporters, who continued to linger at their home, looking for a story. "But we are trying to bear up under this tragedy as bravely as possible."

THE "FOX'S" CONFESSION

Hickman was on board the Union Pacific's Cascade Limited, heading toward Los Angeles, when he announced to District Attorney Keyes that he was ready to talk. "I want to tell the whole story," he said. And he did – almost.

No one knows why Hickman's tune changed when he got on board that train. Maybe it was the sudden notoriety, the cameras, the crowds, or all the attention, but Hickman appeared different once he took his seat on the train to L.A. He suddenly wanted to talk about the kidnapping and murder. This was his chance to be in the spotlight and just as he had relished the attention that he got from the reporters who wanted to take his picture when he was brought into the Pendleton jail, he now had the full attention of veteran police officers and the Los Angeles District Attorney. With a pen and pad of paper in hand, he wanted to make the most of it.

He began his narrative reiterating that the only reason that he came up with the idea of kidnapping and holding a child for ransom was so that he could raise the money to go back to college. He wrote it as though this excused the heinous acts that he committed. He had already been in touch with President Hawley of Park College in Kansas City, he wrote, justifying whatever he needed to do to make that happen.

Hickman finally admitted that he acted alone in the kidnapping and murder of Marion Parker. In November, he had rented the apartment at the Bellevue Arms under the assumed name of "Donald Evans," but he didn't come up with the plans for the kidnapping until December 12. At that point, he planned to try and kidnap the child of Harry Hovis, the Chief Teller at the First National Bank. Hickman wrote: "But I wasn't satisfied with the situation. I then thought of P.M. Parker because I had seen a young girl with him one day at the bank while I was employed there. I decided to start with my plans."

Hickman again stated that he had scouted the Parker house, followed Marion and Marjorie to school, and attempted to lure them from the streetcar. He also admitted to lying to Mary Holt about an accident and convincing her to let him take Marion from the school. "There was only a slight wait and Marion was called from class," he wrote. "I told her to come with me, repeating what I had said to the teacher. The young girl did not hesitate to come with me and we left school immediately."

After driving through the city, the car eventually ended up in Glendale. It was then that Hickman told Marion that she had been deceived. He said that he just planned to hold her for a day or two, until he could convince her father to give him $1,500. Marion didn't cry, or try to fight, Hickman said, but she did ask not to be blindfolded or tied up. She promised not to move or say anything. Hickman showed her a revolver and warned her that he would have to hurt her if she tried to get away. Marion understood. She didn't want to be shot.

Hickman continued his narrative. They drove back to Los Angeles and to the main post office. He said, "I mailed a special delivery letter to Marion's father. Marion sat right up in the seat beside me and talked in a friendly manner. It was very nice to hear her and I could see that she believed and trusted me for her safety."

They drove to Pasadena, where Hickman sent the first telegram to Parker. He warned him not to do anything until he received the letter and assured him that his daughter was safe. At that point, she probably was. Hickman told investigators, "We talked and had a jolly time. Marion said she liked to go driving and she went so far as to relate to me that she had a dream just a few days before that someone called for her at school and, in reality, kidnapped her. Before dark came I turned back and we stopped in Alhambra where I mailed a second telegram.

After that, the two attending a showing of the film *Figures Don't Lie* at the Rialto Theater in South Pasadena. They enjoyed the picture, Hickman said, and they laughed a lot during the opening vaudeville act. After the movie was out, he took Marion to his place at the Bellevue Arms. They had to wait almost a half hour in the car before he could sneak her in without anyone seeing her. She went to sleep on the couch and didn't stir until 7:00 the next morning. Hickman said that he stayed awake for some time to see that Marion didn't try to leave the apartment. When he was convinced she was sound asleep, he drifted off himself.

Early the next morning, Hickman tried to make Marion breakfast, but she said she wasn't hungry. She was crying and upset. "After a while I began to talk to Marion and tried to console her. I told her she could write a letter to her father and that I would also," he said. It's very unlikely that Marion had any idea about the contents of the letter that her abductor had written. If she had, she would not have been consoled.

While he was away from the apartment to mail the letters, he tied Marion to a chair with cloth bandages. He stated that she was not upset and that he did not blindfold or gag her because she promised to stay quiet. After he returned, they went driving again. They stayed on the road until dark and at one point, a gas station attendant in Santa Ana looked very closely at Marion. Hickman feared that she had been recognized, but the attendant never said anything.

Hickman's mugshot – the face of a monster, disguised as a young man who would "never hurt anyone."

They returned to Los Angeles around 7:00 p.m. Hickman tried a few times to reach Perry Parker by telephone, but the line was busy. They drove some more. At a drugstore near Sister Aimee Semple McPherson's Angeles Temple, he called again and this time was able to speak with Parker. He said that he had the money and wanted his daughter back. Hickman ended the call with a promise to call back in five minutes, but it was nearly 30 minutes later when he called from a drug store at Pico and Wilton Streets. They made plans to meet and exchange Marion for the money.

But, of course, things didn't go as planned on Friday night. Hickman later wrote: "Marion and I were parked on Pico between Wilton and Gramercy and we both saw Mr. Parker drive by. There were two other cars following his and I feared some detectives were planning to trap me so Marion and I drove directly back to my apartment and didn't go by her father."

Hickman was angry and in the morning, after Marion woke from a second night in a strange place, he told her to write her father and to tell him that he must not try and trap Hickman – or something might happen to her. Marion agreed and Hickman told investigators that she knew he had written in his letters that he planned to kill her if the ransom wasn't paid. "But she knew I didn't mean it," Hickman said, "and was not worried or excited about it. In fact, I promised that even though her father didn't pay me the money, I would let her go unharmed. She felt perfectly safe."

Hickman wrote his third letter and put it with Marion's note in the same envelope. He was going to mail it, he told her, and then would come back and get her and they would take the car to meet her father somewhere that morning. I tied her to a chair again, just as he had on Friday morning, except that he blindfolded her this time. As he started to walk out the door, Marion called to him to hurry and come back.

"At this moment, my intention to murder completely gripped me."

Hickman didn't walk out the door. He went into the kitchen and picked up a rolling pin that he was going to hit her with. He changed his mind. He took a dish towel instead. He placed it around Marion's neck and mumbled that she could rest her head on it. And then he pulled it around her throat and used all of his strength to choke her. She made no sound, other than a wheezing gasp for air, and then she slumped over in silence.

When her body stopped thrashing, he untied the bandages and laid her on the floor. Her body was taken to the bathtub and then he began to cut. Once the body had been dismembered, she was carefully prepared. The twisted creation – which, hours later, would be revealed to the horror of Perry Parker – was placed in a suitcase, which was then carried to a shelf in the dressing room while Hickman cleaned up the bloody mess he had made.

Believing that every trace of gore had been removed from the apartment, he sat down at his desk and wrote a second part to this third letter, which he called the "final change terms." It was mailed that afternoon and then he went to see a movie at the Loew's State Theater.

Hickman said, "But I was unable to keep my mind on the picture and wept during the performance."

He returned home at 5:30 p.m. He gathered all of the parts of Marion's body and took them to his car, which he had parked at the side entrance. He set off for Elysian Park, where he scattered the limbs and the girl's internal organs.

A half hour later, he continued his grim mission. He took the suitcase with the upper section of the corpse and drove to Sixth Street and Western Avenue. He called Mr. Parker and arranged to meet him. He waited and then drove around the neighborhood to make sure that no police cars were prowling the nearby streets. When he decided that he was safe, he took the dead girl's torso from the suitcase. He propped it up on the seat of his car and bundled the blanket around her so that she would not fall over. Her eyes had been stitched open so that it would look like she was alive.

After the ransom meeting, collecting the money, and dumping the body next to the road, he went to dinner at Leighton's Café, where he used the first of the $20 gold certificates to pay for his meal. After dinner, he returned home to his apartment and went to bed. He slept soundly until morning. Aside from his claim that he "wept" during the movie he saw on Saturday night, he was apparently never really bother by the horrific events that he had carried out.

Hickman signed his confession, which was also signed by the lawmen and Hickman's guards, Chief Davis, Dwight Longuevan, Harry Raymond, Dick Lucas, George Home, and District Attorney Asa Keyes.

It was a story of torture, death, and depravity that was so disturbing that even some of the hard-bitten and experienced detectives who had gathered to hear the tale were sick to their stomachs.

But Hickman wasn't done yet. There was still more to tell.

Hickman wanted more paper. He wanted to add to his statement and clarify for the prosecutor why he had killed Marion. He had good reasons, and he wanted the investigators to understand them.

He started his second confession, "In the first place let me say that the only circumstances connecting my intentions of murder to Marion Parker are purely incidental. I was not prompted by revenge in the killing of Marion Parker. Only through my association with Mr. P.M. Parker at the First National Bank while I worked there as a page from January to June 1927, made it possible for me to see Marion Parker and to know she was P.M.

Parker's daughter. This was incidental and I merely picked it up and followed it through."

Hickman made a list of reasons for the murder, starting with his fear of detection by the police. He believed that if he killed her and dissected the body, he could evade suspicion and arrest. He blamed Perry Parker for not following his directions and keeping the case a secret. If he had, well, the murder might not have happened. He claimed, "After successfully dodging the authorities for two days, I was overcome by such fear that I did not hesitate even to murder to escape notice."

After blaming the murder first on Perry Parker, he then shifted the blame to Marion herself. He said that while he knew that Marion depended on him to keep his word and return her to her family even if her father didn't pay, Hickman felt that his need to secure the money and return to college was more important. He noted, "I knew that if I refused to take her back on Saturday she might distrust me enough to give some sign which would cause my discovery." So, in order for Hickman to go through with his plans to get the money and keep Marion from being disappointed in him, he killed her. But, of course, he did it "so suddenly and unexpectedly that she never had a fear or thought of her own death," he claimed. Hickman added that he only cut her up so that he could get her out of his apartment without anyone seeing him.

It wasn't because he had the urge to cut up the body – or was it?

His final reason for the murder was simply, well, because he had always wanted to kill someone. Although he had always lived his life on the straight and narrow path, he had "an uncontrollable desire to commit a great crime." Hickman, despite the claims that he had already made and would continue to make at trial, insisted that he was not insane, but that his urge was a form of mental illness. He just couldn't help it. He should feel a terrible guilt over Marion's murder, he said, but instead, "felt that some kind of providence was guiding and protecting me in this whole case."

He had simply not been able to stop himself, he said, it was out of his hands. He blamed the murder on those impulses – and also on Perry Parker and his murdered daughter – but Hickman himself hadn't been able to stop it from happening.

Hickman's confessions did not have anything to do with guilt. The detectives saw how much he enjoyed writing his accounts, carefully choosing the correct words. He wrote, rewrote, added notes, and carefully worded the accounts so that he appeared to have given them great thought. He was proud of the finished product as he had been with his performances during the debate contests of his high school days.

Hickman's statements were widely published in newspapers across the country. The public was alternately fascinated, angered, outraged, and repulsed by the words of the monster who had murdered and dismembered an innocent 12-year-old girl. Marion Parker had achieved a tragic infamy, and now a vengeful nation wanted justice to be served.

The editors and reporters who published news of Hickman and his confessions were as sickened as the public. One of the writers who covered the Parker case was Edgar Rice Burroughs, the popular creator of the Tarzan books that had recently been made into motion pictures. Burroughs, covering the case for the *Los Angeles Examiner*, called Hickman a "moral imbecile" and said that he was a "new species of man, differentiated by something other than anatomical divergences."

There were also editorials that blamed Hickman's crime on the influence of Hollywood movies. The 1920s were an era that saw a rise in popularity of feature films and Hollywood had already endured several scandals – from rape cases to drug overdoses – by the time that Hickman committed his crime. It was easy to blame the movies, much in the same way that future generations would blame crimes on television, comic books, and video games. A *New York Times* article stated, "The motion picture screen for the past twenty-five years has been a school for crime." It added that movies were also a menace to children and a furtherance of world peace. However, while Hickman loved movies, he also loved opera, and to say that films had any impact on his gruesome actions was to accept that opera was just as responsible.

There were no movies, magazines, or radio shows that could be blamed for the murder of Marion Parker. The blame rested squarely on the shoulders of William Edward Hickman, who quickly began to enjoy his "celebrity status" – as twisted as that status might be. At each of the train's stops, there were hundreds of curious gawkers. Hickman pressed his face to the window, trying to recognize faces from previous stops.

He had resigned himself to the fact that he had been captured. Now he had to use the situation to his advantage. He was a master criminal who had finally committed his "great crime." Now he had to make himself famous.

Chief Herman Cline was well aware of the crowds that would be meeting the train when it arrived in Los Angeles. He feared there would be trouble. To some, Hickman was some sort of perverse folk hero and a group of his "fans" would undoubtedly be in the crowd. Just as likely, there would be just as many – or more – people there who wanted to kill him. Angry crowds easily turned into angry mobs, more than willing to drag Hickman off the train and lynch him from the closest light pole. As happy as Cline would have probably been to see Hickman dead, he had a duty to let justice have its way with the confessed killer. He planned to deliver him safely to the jail and the best way to do that was to make sure that Hickman never got anywhere near the train station.

On December 27, as the train drew closer to the city, Hickman, awakened at 3:00 a.m., was dressed, and was fed his breakfast while the police officers made plans to slip their prisoner safely into the city.

The newspapers reported on a frenzy that gripped the city. Restrictions had been tightened as the train neared Los Angeles. Doors were bolted and railroad detectives were used to guard the tracks. At Glendale, a crowd of more than 1,000 people crowded the rail line, trying to catch a glimpse of the "Fox." The train did not stop. It paused at Jackson and Alameda Streets and when it did, detectives guarding the heavily shackled prisoner jumped with him from the train and dashed toward five waiting police cars. In seconds, the procession sped off for the county jail – where another 4,000 people were waiting. The crowd, as one large mass, moved toward Hickman. Police officers had to push the onlookers back with force. As the guards brought him into the building, Hickman ducked behind the burly officers, crouching down between them as the seething mob shouted his name.

He probably wasn't feeling quite so happy to be famous at that point.

Five minutes later, at 10:15 a.m., Hickman was securely behind bars. His cell was on the tenth floor of the jail and he was fitted with a heavy ball and chain to dissuade any thoughts of escape. He was heavily guarded and his cell had extra security locks and its own built-in alarm. It was meant to be used for the most extreme criminals.

In just over an hour, he found himself facing Superior Court Judge Carlos Hardy, who informed him that his arraignment had been postponed until 2:00 p.m. the next afternoon, when his attorney was expected to arrive.

Hickman (just left of center) at his hearing in the courtroom. His arraignment was postponed until his attorney arrived. Hickman told reporters that he planned to plead guilty, no matter what his attorney might tell him to do.

While Hickman's train had been en route to Los Angeles, his mother, Eva, had telegraphed the court from Kansas City to announce that she had retained attorney Jerome Walsh to represent her son. Walsh was only 25-years-old, but he was the son of Frank P. Walsh, one of the most legendary lawyers in the Midwest. Apparently, the young attorney, anxious to make a name for himself, had accepted the Hickman case for no fee. He had left Kansas City for L.A. that morning and was expected to arrive the next day.

The *Los Angeles Times* painted a vivid picture of the scene that morning:

The courtroom scene attendant upon Hickman's session was one seldom matched in local court history. News that Hickman had been lodged in jail and would be taken before Judge Hardy for arraignment spread through the building and out onto the street as if by magic, despite the precautions taken by the officers and the speed with which they worked.

Deputy sheriffs and a small army of uniformed officers from the city, and the county motorcycle squad were hurried up to the eighth floor of the Hall of Justice, where the courtroom is located. They filled the courtroom.

They filled the corridors. They guarded elevators and they guarded all entrances and exits.

Hickman, not surprisingly, thrived on the attention. The same thing that occurred after his arrest in Pendleton repeated itself in Los Angeles – the seemingly cowed and frightened and he began playing the boastful "master criminal" that he fancied himself to be. After his court appearance, Hickman was returned to his cell and he spoke to reporters.

"I'll plead guilty and stand by my confession regardless of what my attorney advises me to do," he announced with a hint of swagger in his tone. He told reporters that he was ready to face the consequences of his actions.

A reporter asked, "Suppose your attorney advises you to plead not guilty and stand trial?"

"I would plead guilty anyhow," Hickman sneered.

"You want a speedy trial?"

"Yes, I want a speedy trial." Then after a pause, he added, "But not too speedy."

Hickman even agreed to meet with Perry Parker if asked to do so, promising that he would tell him everything in great detail. Hickman's interest in bragging about his exploits even extended to the mournful father of his young victim. This announcement did not have the intended effect on the reporters – even the most jaded of them were appalled.

Eva Hickman was also talking to the press. She insisted that he was only a tool and was convinced that her "good boy" couldn't have done such a terrible thing. She continued to believe that Ed was only carrying out a scheme and was being directed by an accomplice, who was the real killer.

Meanwhile, in El Paso, Texas, Hickman's father was also speaking to the press. "Since he had confessed to this awful crime, I've disowned him as my son and am content to let the law have him. I was hopeful William was telling the truth when he said that he had not murdered the child. Kidnapping was bad enough. Now I want to see him punished according to the crime."

But Hickman's attorney, Jerome Walsh, had other ideas. Rumors were circulated that he planned to have his client plead not guilty by reason of insanity. The editors at the *Times* had their own thoughts about this latest development. "Society does not have to give up restraining criminals merely because a psychologist thinks he had discovered they are machines instead of beings with wills, souls and consciences. A dog that becomes dangerous is either muzzled or shot, according to the circumstances, and no inquiry is made as to whether or not he is "responsible."

THE "FOX" ON TRIAL

On December 28, Hickman was officially arraigned for the kidnapping and murder of Marion Parker. Attorney Walsh, citing his need to become intimately familiar with the details of the "gruesome affair," requested a continuance be granted until Tuesday, January 3, when he would enter a plea on his client's behalf. Judge Hardy granted the delay.

Unhappy with the delay, the newspapers went looking for a story – and soon found one. On December 29, 16-year-old Welby Hunt, who was also from Kansas City and was a "pal" of Hickman, confessed to authorities that he had been involved with Hickman in a string of armed robberies. The robberies included one at the Rose Hill Pharmacy on Christmas Eve 1926, during which Hickman shot the proprietor, C. Ivy Thoms, to death.

The *Times* jumped on the story: "The Thoms murder confession came as a startling climax to Hickman's revolting statement admitting the murder and mutilation of little Marion Parker, whom he kidnapped from school two weeks ago. Hunt's confession, in which he admitted being present at the time of the shooting but denied firing the shot that killed Thoms, added another chapter to the amazing orgy of crime directed during the past year by the brutal slayer of the Parker girl."

Things looked even worse when Hunt told the police that Hickman had spoken to him of "cutting up someone." Apparently he told his friend, "he had always had a desire to cut up someone and throw them along the highway." Hunt said that he dismissed this as just idle talk, noting that Hickman was "occasionally moody and silly, but not sick or insane."

Hickman readily admitted to the Thoms robbery. At this point, he was admitting to pretty much everything he had ever done. His first few days in lockup were filled with visits from various analysts, all wanting some of his time. Hickman obliged. His sporadic behavior, inconsistent attitude, and the fact that he had committed a horrible crime led most people to believe he was insane – but not the doctors. He had carefully explained his crime and realized that he was going to pay the price for it. Hickman wasn't playing the crazy act that he'd tried in Oregon, at least not at first. He seemed lucid and understanding of his actions. This led the doctors who examined him to believe that he was in control of his mental facilities.

It wasn't a doctor that Hickman spoke about the Thoms robbery with -- it was one of his many guards, jailer Frank Dewar. They were making small talk at about 4:00 a.m. and Dewar asked him about the news story. Hickman asked for a pen and paper – he wanted to write it all down – and began scrawling an account of the robbery, including the cop on the beat who wandered into the pharmacy and was wounded in the shootout when Hickman and Hunt made their escape. Dewar immediately got the written confession to the Homicide Bureau, and a short time later, Hunt was picked up on suspicion of murder.

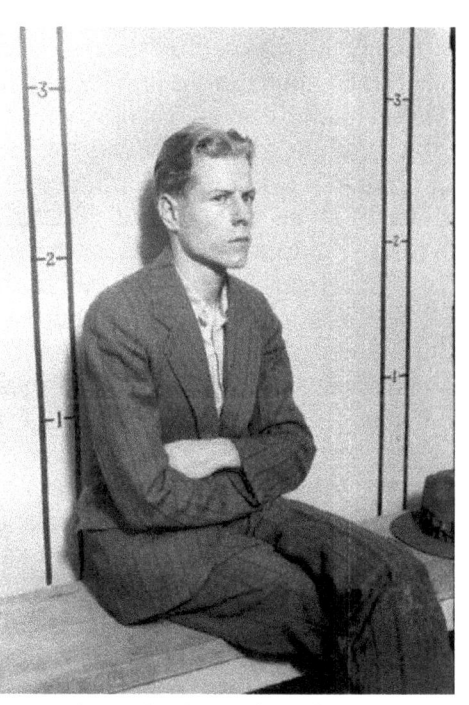

Hickman's friend and former stickup partner, Welby Hunt, who was 16-years-old at the time of his arrest, which spared him a chance to go to the gallows.

Hunt wasn't worried at first, but he should have been. He admitted to being part of the holdup, but said he never fired a shot. He had been carrying a .38-caliber gun and his now infamous partner had been carrying a .32. Hunt should have waited to hear about the autopsy report on Ivy Thomas – he'd been killed by a .38. Now, charged with murder, people started to wonder if Hunt might have also been Hickman's accomplice in the Marion Parker murder also. But Hickman insisted that he acted alone and that he had no contact with Hunt at the time. Even so, Hunt found himself charged with murder and another charge was added to Hickman's roster of felonies.

Welby Hunt's mother naturally defended her son in the press: "I know my son is innocent. He is a good boy, and I am certain this merely is Edward Hickman's means of retaliating. From the very first, when reports came from California that my son had given aid to the police, I was afraid of what Hickman might do. At first I was afraid he might return to kill my boy as he killed Marion Parker. Then, when he was captured, I thought my boy would be safe. But now I see I was mistaken."

Hunt's mother stuck up for her son in the papers the same way that Eva Hickman defended Ed. But Ed confessed to both crimes and named Welby Hunt, and now it was up to the police and the courts to sort it out.

But things got murkier before that happened.

It was soon discovered that Hunt and Hickman had been together at the time that Hunt's grandfather, A.R. Driskell, committed suicide. There had always been some skepticism about the suicide notes that Driskell left behind. In light of the news about the Thoms murder – combined with the Marion Parker tragedy – the police started delving in Driskell's death all over again. A handwriting expert went over the suicide notes and there turned out to be a series of tangible similarities between those notes and the letters that Hickman wrote to Perry Parker as the "Fox." Perhaps Driskell didn't commit suicide after all.

The press ripped into the Welby Hunt story and then exploded with accounts of Hickman's past. As he casually told of his exploits, they were snatched up by the nation's newspapers and printed them for all to read. Hickman was a small-time stickup man. He was already a murderer before he ever met Perry or Marion Parker. Hickman acted alone in his murder and dismemberment of an innocent child. He was sane according to prison psychiatrists. And the stories, articles, and editorials went on and on.

The notoriety that Hickman was attaining with the public was reflected among the other prisoners in the jail. A photograph of Hickman was suspended from his cell door by a string, fashioned into a hangman's noose. Guards confiscated broom handles that had been broken off and turned into clubs. Hickman was the intended victim of a beating. When he was escorted past another cell and made eye contact or smirked at another prisoner, they glared at him with the same murderous intensity that had come from the mobs at the train station. Unlike the ordinary people who met the train, though, the prisoners were fully capable of murder. Hickman had to be closely guarded at all times.

Hickman was living in fear and decided to write a letter to his mother to try and take his mind off things. It was the first time that he had communicated with her since his arrest. He wanted to console her – but he still couldn't help but boast about his "great crime." He wrote:

> Dear Mother,
> I certainly appreciate your kind letter and I want you to know that I still care for you. It's so sweet of you to be willing to help, no matter what has happened, and your love is simply overwhelming. I have no fear of what may come. I have been truthful and confessed everything. Everyone has treated me nice. I have slept well and feel in perfect health. In spite of everything people can't help but sympathize with me and praise you for your strong mother love. After talking with me and being around me, people can't realize my guilt, but it is so, nevertheless. Mr. Gustave R. Briegleb of St. Paul's Presbyterian Church gave me a Bible and I am reading it some. I like the Psalms and seem to get real comfort out of them. God bless you, Mother. May He comfort you and see the whole thing through to the end.
>
> Your son,
> Edward Hickman

Hickman in his cell at the Los Angeles County Jail – this was obviously a photo that was staged for reporters.

While Hickman was writing letters to his mother and trying to stay alive in jail, his attorney, Jerome Walsh, was working to gather material for his client's insanity defense. He believed in its success. He would be using the same methods that had worked so well for Clarence Darrow a few years before in Chicago, when he had saved the lives of Leopold and Loeb.

Hickman's legal problems were continuing in another case. He and Welby Hunt had just been indicted by a grand jury for the murder of Ivy Thoms. His widow had identified them both in a lineup. Hickman again pleaded insanity. Hunt said nothing. He was just 16 and could not be executed for his crime, but he could get life in prison. However, Hickman had two murders that could send him to the gallows.

Jerome Walsh had his work cut out for him.

On January 3, 1928, Hickman, who with much bravado had claimed he would plead guilty to kidnapping and murder no matter what his attorney told him to do, entered a plea of not guilty by reason of insanity. Jerome Walsh had filed an affidavit asking for a delay in entering his client's plea, but this was denied. After Hickman's plea was entered, Walsh again asked for a delay of 35 days, which was five days over the state's legal limit. Judge Hardy noted that Walsh had no probable witnesses in his affidavit and set a trial date for January 25.

The trial would serve two purposes – it would be a legal trial and a sanity hearing in which life or death figured in the balance. If the jury found Hickman to be guilty and sane, he would go to the gallows. If, however, the jury ruled that he was guilty and insane, he would spend the rest of his life in the State Hospital for the Criminally Insane. However, if the latter verdict was rendered, there was yet another wrinkle. If at any time during his confinement at the state hospital, it could be determined that his sanity had returned, he would then be sentenced to death.

As soon as Hickman was returned to his holding cell at the county jail to await his trial, his attorney, and a deputy district attorney, left town to seek out witnesses, statements, and affidavits about Hickman's past. Both men took the same Santa Fe train, bound for Kansas City. It was a quick turnaround trip for Walsh.

In jail, Hickman enthusiastically embraced his role as an insane person. Whenever jail officers or officials connected to his trial were present, the normally outgoing and boastful inmate would suddenly become catatonic, staring at the walls of his cell for hours. Other times, he babbled incoherently or howled and barked like a dog. Other inmates, appalled by his horrible crimes and disgusted by his antics, strung a large photograph of Hickman over a rafter. They punched a hole on either side, placed a rope about his neck, and hanged Hickman in effigy.

Meanwhile, plans were being made for Hickman to be tried along with Welby Hunt for the murder of Ivy Thoms. Hunt's attorney had already announced that his client would plead guilty, causing some to speculate that Hunt may have agreed to testify against Hickman. In court on January 10, however, Hunt entered a plea of not guilty and his attorney petitioned the court for his client to be tried separately from Hickman, who would stand trial for the murder of Thoms after the completion of the Parker murder trial – unless he was found guilty of capital murder, of course. The judge denied the request and the Thoms murder trial was set for February 15.

Strange things – even stranger than usual -- were happening in the Hickman case. Five days before the trial was scheduled to start, Hickman's father, William Thomas – who initially claimed that he had disowned his son – showed up in Los Angeles to attest to the alleged strain of mental illness that ran through his ex-wife's family. He told reporters, "If placed on the witness stand, I will testify that Edward is suffering from hereditary insanity. I do not think Edward should ever be permitted to walk the streets. He is a dangerous being, and if I felt entirely satisfied as to his mental condition, then I would expect him to pay the supreme penalty. There is no place in this country for such a beast as he has proven to be, except solitary confinement, if insane. If he is sane, then the gallows."

Three days later, Eva Hickman and another her daughter, Mary, arrived in Los Angeles. Eva met at length with her incarcerated son, but refused to pose for photographs with him and declined to speak to the press.

There was also an eerie near encounter that took place in the courtroom during Hickman's arraignment for Marion's murder. During the hearing, he sat next to Walsh, looking down at the floor and only speaking twice. After entering his plea, Hickman was asked if he knew that his insanity plea constituted an admission of the murder. He said that he did. At the rear of the courtroom – less than a dozen yards away – sat Perry Parker, Jr., Marion's older brother and the sole representative of the Parker family at the arraignment. He was laying eyes on Hickman for the first time and reporters closely watched his reaction. He appeared to be very tense, and under a great deal of strain. Reporters recalled that his eyes rapidly darted back and forth between the judge and the man who had killed and dismembered his beloved little sister. When the arraignment ended and Hickman was taken from the room, Parker offered no comments to the reporters who clamored around him and shouted questions. He walked out of the courtroom without uttering a word.

The prosecution had already stated that Perry's long-suffering father would be participating in the trial. Mr. Parker was not looking forward to it. His cherished daughter was dead, she would not be coming home, and her killer was in the custody of the police. He simply wanted the justice system to do its part and sentence Hickman to death.

However, he knew the importance of his role in the trial. He would not be cross-examined, and he could be brief and to the point. Parker mulled it over for a long time and discussed it with his son, still shielding his wife and his surviving daughter from the horrifying details. After a long period of conflicting thoughts and mixed feelings, Perry Parker agreed to testify against Hickman. He had done it once before, of course, but this time was something much more serious than forgery at the bank.

Mary Hickman, who lived with her mother and was "stunned" by the revelation that her brother was the "Fox."

Jerome Walsh, Hickman's attorney, was not working alone in the sensational case. He was assisted by Richard Cantillon, who would later write a book about the trial – and the horror that he felt when he first heard about Marion Parker's brutal murder. Cantillon had a child of his own, and another on the way. He could not imagine the pain being felt by Perry Parker. But he believed that there was no way that Hickman could possibly be sane. He thought that the very act of killing and dismembering a young girl was reason enough to believe that Hickman was insane and he agreed to work on the case to make sure that Hickman's rights were not violated. He felt it was his duty as an attorney and an officer of the court – no matter how he might personally feel about his client and the horrible things that he'd done.

After being hired to work with Walsh, Cantillon generated a flurry of paperwork and motions. The first was to ask for a change of venue for the trial. He told reporters, "All Los Angeles County are biased and prejudiced against the defendant." By this time, most people in the entire country hated Hickman, but Cantillon believed that Los Angeles County was the worst possible place for his client to get a fair trial. Walsh agreed with him and Cantillon filed the motion on January 13. The motion was denied.

Walsh and Cantillon were undaunted. After losing their motion for a change of venue, they went looking for other ways to delay the January 25 start to the trial. They spent the next 10 days researching every aspect of the case, including finding doctors who would testify on behalf of Hickman and state that he was insane. As part of their research, Walsh and Cantillon extensively interviewed Hickman. He included all of the details that he gave to Chief Cline, the horrors that were chronicled in his written confession – and more. Once again, Hickman added to his story, unleashing depravity not yet realized, along with some possible lies and exaggerations. It was hard for anyone to know where truth ended and legends began with the unnerving young man.

According to Hickman, Marion had actually enjoyed her kidnapping at first. She thought of it as an adventure, he claimed. Hickman gave her candy bars and let her play his phonograph. He had an impressive collection of jazz and popular records and one of them, *Pretty Baby*, was her favorite song and she played it over and over again. Hickman really liked Marion. She was cute, had a sparkling personality, and a good sense of humor.

Neither of them were focusing on the situation they were in. It's likely that both of them thought it would all be over soon. Perry Parker would pay the ransom and Marion would go home. For Hickman, this was his "great crime" and it would net him the money he needed to go back to college. Marion had been easily taken, she was no bother, the ransom would be paid, and he would get away with it. Marion was having an adventure and it was exciting and non-threatening enough that she didn't have time to think about how much danger she was in. By evening, she'd be home, she thought.

On Saturday morning, though, the day after the failed ransom exchange, Marion no longer saw her abduction as some sort of lark. Hickman had been promising her that if she cooperated, she would be home with her family Friday night. She had cooperated, but after the police were spotted nearby, Hickman could not make the exchange without getting arrested. The plan fell apart, but Marion was a child who wanted her parents. It wasn't an adventure anymore. She wanted to go home, she became upset, and she started to cry.

Marion was no longer the cute, funny child whose company Hickman had enjoyed. She was now angry, frightened, confused, and troublesome. With all of these qualities making her much less interesting, she started to bother Hickman. Becoming hysterical, he wasn't able to console her and he started to get impatient and irritated. Through her tears, Marion demanded to be taken home. He tried to reason with her, carefully explaining that he would be arrested. She didn't care. She wanted to go home and she wanted Hickman to go away and leave her and her family alone. Forget about the ransom, forget about the police, just drop her off somewhere and let her walk away. She wasn't having fun anymore; she was scared. Marion was relentless. She refused to eat and spent all of Saturday crying. When she finally fell asleep, it was due to exhaustion.

Hickman's new story had begun to skew wildly away from the written confession he had made on the train. He had claimed that Marion was comfortably tied up when he was preparing to leave and take a note to Mr. Parker. He also wrote that she had asked him to "hurry back," and it was then that the urge to kill her gripped him. But, according to what he told Cantillon, this was not the case.

Hickman did not leave a comfortable, unknowing child who promised to be quiet. He admitted to his lawyers that he lifted her sleeping body and put her into the chair, tied her tightly, shoved a handkerchief into her mouth, and gagged her with a dishtowel so that she wouldn't scream. Marion woke up as he was tying her and she began to scream through the cloth, struggled against the bindings. Hickman left her alone, bound and gagged, in a pitch-dark apartment while he sent another letter to her father.

When Hickman returned, he found Marion screaming through her gag, trying to free herself, and struggling to breathe. Her eyes were wide with terror. Hickman told his lawyers that when he saw her eyes, her felt immediate remorse. He very briefly considered setting her free, dropping her off in front of her house, and fleeing the state. But then he realized that as soon as she was free, Marion would start to scream, and he'd never get away.

Hickman wanted the ransom money. He wanted to go to college, where he would study to be a minister. He felt called by God. He said that he prayed for guidance and, as he did, he saw a vision of an elderly man who commanded him to strangle Marion. Kill her, the man told him. Hickman told his attorneys that he had to obey. He demanded of Cantillon, "If God asked you to do something, wouldn't you do it?"

Hickman untied the dish towel that was holding in the gag and Marion looked up at him with trusting eyes. She apparently believed that he was about to set her free. Hickman was going to take her home. Was it finally over?

And then Hickman wrapped the dish towel around her throat and pulled with all his strength. Marion struggled and then her body went limp. Hickman sat down on the couch and he stared at her stillness until the sun came up.

What was he going to do with the body?

Richard Cantillon was shocked into silence by Hickman's description of the murder. It included much more than what was in his highly-publicized written confession. They were details that no one else had heard, especially the police and the prosecution. And he wasn't finished. His story continued, becoming even more gruesome and horrifying. He spared no details. Hickman likely felt that he needed to tell everything if his attorneys were truly going to do their best to build his insanity defense.

If that was the case, it worked. Cantillon already believed that Hickman was insane. By the time he was finished with his account, he was also convinced that he was a monster.

While Marion's body was lying in the apartment, Hickman went out to purchase makeup and lipstick. The girl at the counter was amused and wondered what a man could possibly want with women's cosmetics. Hickman smiled, but did not answer her.

When he returned home, he pondered how to remove Marion's body from his apartment without it being seen. The only container that he had that was large enough was a suitcase. But to fit in the suitcase, he would have to cut her apart.

He untied her body and placed it on the couch. He used a golf club to measure the length, width, and depth of the body and did the same for the suitcase. Marion was stripped and placed face down in the bathtub. He tied towel strips around her ankles and hoisted the body up over the drain, using the towel rack. As her lifeless corpse hung naked over the tub, he recalled a job that he had once had on a poultry farm, disemboweling and disjointing chickens. He put that practical knowledge to use. He pulled back on Marion's hair and used a butcher knife to slice open her throat. Turning on the bath water, he watched as her blood swirled down the drain. While this was happening, he went into the kitchen for a snack. When he returned, he moved the body onto the floor, cut into the abdomen, and removed the viscera. The smell that rushed out at him caused him to vomit.

But he was intent on his task. He washed the torso in the tub and then cut through the lower part of it through the backbone. As he did this, the corpse jerked with such force that it flew out of the tub and onto the wet tile floor. Hickman was shaken, but undeterred. He washed and dried the body and then carried the upper part of the torso into the bedroom. He had to cradle the head so that it did not become detached.

Hickman had plenty of newspapers. He had been buying them up so that he could read about his exploits in the headlines. Now, he used the papers to wrap the body parts. In five bundles, he tied each leg, each arm, and the lower torso. They were placed in his bedroom closet with the wrapped viscera. After, he cleaned up the bathroom and then took a bath.

When he was finished, he dressed the largest part of Marion's body that remained. He slipped her dress over the head and torso. Her face was white, so he used the cosmetics that he had purchased to put some color back in her cheeks. He then pierced the upper eyelids with a needle, inserted a thin thread that was nearly invisible, and hooked it over the outside of the lid. Marion's eyes were sewn opened into a gaping stare. He was careful not to pull the thread too taut – he wanted her to look like she was awake, not frightened.

Her hair was pulled into a ponytail and her hair ribbon was steamed and held against a lightbulb so that it appeared newly pressed. A bow was tied around the ponytail. He knew that it would be dark when he returned Marion to her father, but he wanted Perry Parker to believe she was alive. He figured that Parker would ask to see her before he handed over the money.

Marion was ready to be returned to her father.

The rest of Hickman's story didn't differ from the written account, but Richard Cantillon was sickened and disturbed by his client's graphic tale. Everything about his meeting with Perry Parker was told in the same way, but Hickman did have more to say about what happened next. Hickman had been making claims about his encounter with police officers after the kidnapping while he was in jail in Oregon. As mentioned, there is no evidence to say that this actually happened, but Hickman did tell the story again to his attorneys as they prepared for the trial. Hickman told so many stories, then altered them, that it was hard to know how much of what he said was the truth.

After murdering and dismembering Marion and delivering a portion of her body to Perry Parker in exchange for the $1,500, Hickman said that he returned to his apartment. The place was in disarray. Broken golf clubs – that he had used to measure the body and the suitcase – were strewn about, clothes were scattered around, and dishes were in the sink and on the table. Hickman wasn't interested in cleaning up. He needed to get out of town.

Behind him, there was a knock at the door. Hickman asked who it was and "police officers!" was the reply. Hickman claimed that he kept his cool – one of the most unbelievable parts of the story – and asked them to wait a moment. He gathered the ransom money and stashed it behind an ironing board that was built into the wall. He then ran into the bathroom and flushed the toilet. Finally, he opened the door and was met by two detectives. He apologized for the delay, claiming he had been in the bathroom.

The cops entered the apartment – Hickman was registered under the name Donald Evans -- after showing him their badges. They glanced around the messy place and noticed the broken golf clubs on the floor. They asked what had happened to the clubs and Hickman laughed, "After yesterday, I'm never playing that goddamn game again!" The detectives chuckled along with Hickman.

He asked the detectives what they were looking for and they told him that they were checking apartments for clues regarding the fiend that had killed and carved up that little girl. Hickman shook his head, "Wasn't that dreadful?" he asked.

The cops quickly looked around the apartment, glancing in each room, but not checking anything too closely. This was just one of the many apartments in the building. They were all laid out the same and it didn't look any different than the others. Besides, Hickman added, this harmless-looking little man didn't seem the type to hurt anyone – or at least that's what these stupid cops must have thought.

The detectives were satisfied. They spent only a few minutes inside, giving the place a cursory look before deciding to move on. They didn't find anything worth examining further and left the apartment, giving Hickman time to gather his things before escaping from Los Angeles.

Hickman told Cantillon that this incident was further proof that God was watching out for him. To the attorney (and to this author), the story was likely just another way for Hickman to brag about this criminal prowess. He had "put one over on the cops," so to speak. Those dummies had no idea that they had a "criminal mastermind" in their grasp, only to let him slip away. If this incident took place – and it's unlikely that it did – it shows the stress the police were under as they searched wildly for clues in the aftermath of the murder. They must have looked at dozens of apartments that day, saw several dozen men who looked like the description of the kidnapper, and thought nothing of some broken wooden golf clubs, which were easily snapped over a man's knee, even a man as unimpressive as Ed Hickman.

As Cantillon listened to Hickman relate his more detailed account of the murder and dismemberment, he realized how such information could further enflame an angry public. The statements that had already been released to the press were more than enough for the general public to demand Hickman's execution – this could only make things worse. If the more graphic version of events leaked to the press via the courtroom, it would be disastrous to their case. The public wouldn't care if Hickman was insane or not – they'd want him dead.

No one knows why Hickman felt the need to offer another version of events. Perhaps he felt the new details bolstered his chances for an insanity plea – or perhaps he just liked to brag. He wanted to be famous and the bloodier his story became, the more famous he believed he would be.

The one thing that Cantillon knew was that he could never put Hickman on the stand. If he opened his mouth from the witness box, he was guaranteed to hang.

On Wednesday, January 25, the trial of William Edward Hickman – the "Fox" – began in Department 24 of Los Angeles County Superior Court. As reporters jockeyed to find the best seats to cover the proceedings, Judge Hardy arrived in court, a full hour ahead of schedule. There were 50 people waiting to be called as prospective jurors. There were 150 seats available for spectators, but more than 1,000 showed up.

Hickman arrived a few minutes before the proceedings began. He was escorted from his cell to the courtroom by guards armed with tear gas bombs to quell any possible outbreak of violence by the crowd gathered outside. As he entered the courtroom, he made a brief statement to the press. The insanity defense was still planned, but Hickman seemed to be resigned to his fate. "I just want this over and done with," he said. "I'll swing, I know."

Richard Cantillon and Jerome Walsh were still pondering their conversations with Hickman, going over in their minds the gruesome details of Marion's murder and dismemberment. They were convinced that Hickman was insane and were determined to prove it in court.

The courtroom was brought to order at 9:31 a.m. Hickman confessed to murder, with a plea of not guilty by reason of insanity. This was, at the time, a new California law in which the defendant in a case was allowed to state that he was not responsible for his criminal acts because he was insane at the time he committed the crime and did not understand the difference between right and wrong. Hickman would be the first defendant in the state to attempt such a defense.

However, nothing about the day in court went as planned.

Jerome Walsh, who had been attempting to delay the trial from the start, filed a motion that caused a delay. He filed an affidavit that charged Judge Carlos Hardy with prejudice and bias, demanding that a different judge be assigned to conduct the Hickman trial. The motion was based on the fact that Hardy was the presiding judge of the criminal division, and yet he had resigned from that position with the sole purpose of being in charge of Hickman's trial. Whether he had an actual

Defense attorney Jerome Walsh

bias against Hickman, or was simply trying to become famous as the judge who presided over the headline-grabbing case, didn't matter. What mattered was that it looked bad, no matter what the intent. Walsh decided to use that to his advantage. Walsh had Hickman sign and swear to the affidavit in open court, and then Walsh signed it, too. Copies were then given to Judge Hardy and Prosecutor Asa Keyes. Keyes characterized the charges as "the most ridiculous thing I have ever heard."

Court was adjourned until 2:00 p.m. the following day, when Judge Hardy spoke to the assembled attorneys. Denying any prejudice against Hickman, Hardy agreed to step down so that another judge could be appointed to hear the case. Under California law, the defense and prosecuting attorneys were forced to agree on a new judge. Asa Keyes refused to meet with the defense counsel – he was still angry about the complaint against Hardy – but Judge Hardy wanted to move things along and so he disqualified himself from the case, which moved a new judge automatically into his place.

The trial was then taken over by Judge J.J. Trabucco, a visiting judge from Mariposa County. At the time, Trabucco was a 30-year veteran jurist. He had come to Los Angeles to help clear the congested calendar in the local superior court. He suddenly found himself presiding over the "trial of the century," as the press had dubbed it.

The trial was no longer about whether or not Hickman killed Marion. That had been established by his insanity plea. The trial was solely to determine Hickman's sanity when he committed the horrific act. It had to be shown conclusively, beyond a reasonable doubt, that he did not know right from wrong. It had to be proven that he did not understand the consequence of his actions. If his attorneys failed, and he was found to be sane, he would be sentenced for the murder and eventually put to death on the gallows. This was California law at the time. If he was found insane, he would spend the rest of his life in a mental institution – unless his doctors someday decided that he was no longer mentally ill. If that happened, Hickman would still hang.

It was no wonder that he had such a fatalistic outlook toward the trial.

On January 26, at 10:00 a.m., court was back in session. By Friday afternoon, the jurors were in place and when court reconvened on Monday morning, Hickman was sitting at the defense table between his two lawyers, Richard Cantillon and Jerome Walsh. The jury was in the box and had been

The mob scene outside of the courthouse as Hickman's trial was ready to begin. There were only 150 available seats inside the courtroom for the public, but more than 1,000 people showed up to claim them.

sworn in, Judge Trabucco was on the bench, and the trial was finally ready to begin.

Hickman's attorneys, though, had a big problem. The former star of his high school debate team was insisting that he wanted to take the stand in his own defense. He wanted the spotlight. He had wanted to commit a "great crime" and he had, and since he didn't get away with it, he was doing the next best thing – becoming infamous. With this world finally paying attention to him, he wanted to tell everyone what he had done. He wanted to make sure that everyone knew the details of Marion's kidnapping, murder, and dismemberment, just like his attorneys did. He told reporters that he would speak in his own defense, "whether they liked it or not." Walsh and Cantillon knew that if they couldn't talk him out of it, he was doomed.

Walsh spoke to the newsmen himself. "We do not want Hickman to take the witness stand in view of his insanity defense, and we have told him so. Of course, if he is determined to talk we cannot stop him, but such a move would seriously injure defense plans."

Hickman knew that the psychiatrists who had examined him in jail – and were seated in the front row in the courtroom – were studying him and planned to talk about him to the jury. But he believed that, as a master debater, he could sway the jury to his way of thinking, and dismiss what the psychiatrists had to say. He was convinced he was smarter than they were. The trial was just another chance for him to show off his debate skills. His having received honorable mention instead of the top prize in school still angered him. This was his chance to show that he should have won. The courtroom was the ultimate competition. He was on the national stage and his need for attention was just too great to ignore.

Walsh and Cantillon knew that Hickman would not be called to the stand on the first day, so they decided to come up with a strategy that would convince their client that taking the witness stand was not in his best interest. Each time that Hickman recounted the story of Marion Parker's murder, he added more gruesome details. Presenting the account that he had given to his attorneys, in the same relaxed and casual manner, would enrage the public – including the jury. Hickman *must* be kept off the stand.

As the trial was about to start, deputy sheriffs were stationed at the entrances to the courthouse. In those days before metal detectors, the spectators had to be searched for weapons. The jail had received hundreds of letters threatening to kill Hickman. The law was taking no chances that the trial might be cut short by a vigilante's bullet.

At the start of the trial, Judge Trabucco had to explain the new California law about the insanity plea to the jury. Basically, a person could enter a plea of insanity if a diseased or deranged condition of mind rendered them incapable of distinguishing between right and wrong in regards to the act of which they were charged. If someone had an irresistible impulse to commit a crime – but knew it was wrong and unlawful – it did not constitute the legal definition of insanity. In most cases, the burden always fell on the prosecution to show that a defendant was guilty beyond a reasonable doubt, but insanity cases were different. When used as a defense, the burden of proving a defendant insane falls upon his attorney. The defendant had to prove that he was insane when the act took place. This, of course, made an insanity defense much more difficult to pursue – and much harder for those who might be faking the defense to get away with it.

The jury watched Hickman with curiosity. For the most part, he had been stoic throughout all the proceedings as far as the public and press were concerned. Most of his "insanity" antics had occurred in jail. His emotional disruptions were always exhibited away from newspaper reporters and the skeptical eye of the public. Many felt – as Richard Cantillon did – that only an insane person would murder and dismember a child, while others didn't care if Hickman was crazy or not – they just wanted him to pay. The feelings of the jury were not yet clear. The panel was made up of eight men and four women. They were all middle-age and older. It was impossible to know if they would be sympathetic to Hickman's claims, or feel the way that so many people in the country already felt – that he should go to the gallows.

After the court clerk read aloud the indictment against Hickman, the young man's stoicism gave way to nervousness. He fidgeted, squirmed in his chair, and frequently ran a finger around inside of his shirt collar. He knew he was under the watchful eyes of the front-row psychiatrists – and, of course, the jurors. It was almost as if the words of the clerk – noting Hickman's plea of not guilty by reason of insanity – had flipped a switch in his head. A court of law had to be convinced of the fact that he didn't deserve to die. The trial had truly begun and his life was at stake.

The parade of witnesses began, starting with Mary Holt, the school official who had allowed Marion to leave that afternoon with Hickman. The tremendous strain that she had endured since that fateful day had aged her 10 years. Her face was now lined, and her hair had turned white, almost overnight. She had experienced several nervous breakdowns and was under a doctor's care. School administrators had been sympathetic to her, but her work attendance had become sporadic. Most people were supportive of her, even the Parkers, who never spoke out or blamed her for what happened that day. They were too deep in their own grief to try and put the blame on anyone but Ed Hickman.

Mrs. Holt's husband assisted her onto the witness stand. She slowly made it to the chair – looking as though she might collapse – and sat down. With as much tearful composure as she could muster, she identified Hickman in the courtroom and recounted the day that she had made the terrible decision to allow Marion to leave school with him. "I never would have let Marion go but for the apparent sincerity and disarming manner of the man," she wept. She gave as many details as she could, before she began to shake and cry so much that she could barely continue. The lawyers and the judge did not question her for long. Once she was finished, Mrs. Holt and her husband quickly left the courtroom.

Detective George Contreras was the next on the witness stand. He recalled the night that he went to Manhattan Place after receiving an urgent call and finding the devastated Perry Parker and the mutilated remains of his daughter. He told the court, "We searched the automobile and searched the area. When the coroner arrived, I carried the little body out of Parker's car and put it in the dead wagon; then we came down to the morgue with it."

Contreras was a tough veteran detective. He was normally unshakable. He had seen a lot during his days on the job, but the Parker case haunted him. It took a great effort for him to remain unemotional on the stand as he recounted the events of the evening when he was first on the scene, to see Perry Parker just after he discovered his dismembered daughter. And he recalled his first look at Marion, with her dead, staring eyes, with eyelids carefully stitched open. Contreras's toughness was not brittle enough to keep the tears from welling in his eyes.

George Watson, the *Los Angeles Times* photographer who had served on the case in an official capacity for the police, took the stand. He had photographed the coroner's examination of Marion's mutilated remains and the pictures were presented in court and given to the jury for inspection. Eyes widened and faces turned white. The photographs were more gruesome than any of them could have imagined. Members of the jury let out an audible gasp. A female juror leapt to her feet, as though she planned to flee the courtroom. She swayed back and forth for a moment, looking as though she might fall over the railing of the jury box and District Attorney Keyes rushed to her aid. He placed a glass of water in her hand and the woman seated next to her, scarcely in better condition, held the glass as the dazed juror drank. She had to be administered smelling salts to regain her composure. The male jurors looked just as repulsed. Their faces were pale and several of them gritted their teeth and anxiously rubbed their hands together.

Judge Trabucco adjourned court for the day.

The next morning, Hickman's father, William Thomas Hickman, took the stand. This was the start of the defense strategy to prove that insanity ran through Hickman's family.

William Hickman had initially believed that his son should be punished to the fullest extent of the law – and said so in the newspapers. Ed's crime was just too terrible for him to contemplate. But, at some point, Hickman changed his mind, at least somewhat. He had contemplated how a child of his could have committed such a terrible act and had come to the conclusion that it was insanity from Ed's mother's side of the family. So, he wrote a letter to his son's attorneys and offered to try and help save Ed from the noose.

On the stand, Mr. Hickman was questioned by Richard Cantillon. He told about the mental problems that had been suffered by William's mother when he was a boy. She had been locked away in asylums and had attempted suicide. Her breakdowns, he believed, were hereditary. His wife's mother, Rebecca Buck, had also been insane.

When asked to describe the situation, Mr. Hickman replied, "She was of a very melancholy nature, and put in the bigger part of her time crying, it seemed like." He described how she lapsed into spells and always imagined there was something physically wrong with her. Her husband spent hundreds of dollars on medical bills, he thought for no reason. At one point, she became partially paralyzed, convinced it was a serious illness, but doctors could find no cause. She ran in the fields at night, yelling, and would hide so that no one could find her for days. She could never explain why she did those things.

"She had what she called smothering spells," he added, "but it was nothing more than epileptic convulsions, I always thought. She would drop on the floor and, of course, we would all grab her and put her on the bed and start working with her, and work with her until we could bring her out of that. We would keep her from swallowing her tongue, and loosen all her clothing and wipe her face with warm water."

Cantillon then asked him about his ex-wife, Ed's mother, Eva Hickman. "She became just like her mother," he explained. "She would steal herself out nights and sit and cry, and I would get up out of bed and hunt around until I would find her, and finally bring her in the house and try to console her. And she kept that up for a good many years, until after our second child was born, and then she began to get worse."

Mr. Hickman claimed that Eva had a "horror of children, giving birth to children; and married relations, such as sexual relations, she always had a horror to that." This caused a rift in their marriage, which later led to a series of affairs on the part of Mr. Hickman. When Eva did get pregnant, she became unbalanced.

He told Cantillon, "There were times she would threaten me with everything imaginable. She was going to kill me, kill the children, kill herself. She always seemed like she wanted to do some great crime or other. I don't know why. I talked to doctors about her and they would say. 'Oh well, it is just a nervous breakdown; she will come out of it all right."

He went on to say that his wife's problems continued until she was pregnant with Ed. She became so unglued that she would threaten to murder her unborn child "by taking a knife and ripping herself open." She would also threaten that she would murder the children so that Hickman would come home and find their bodies stacked up in a corner of the house.

Eva was at her worst while pregnant with Ed, Hickman said, and she went through 36 hours of labor before the boy was born – stillborn. "He was dead at the time," Hickman said. "The doctors worked with him, for what seemed like an hour before they brought him to. He was just as black as anything you ever saw. I thought he was gone for good."

Cantillon wrapped up his questions and watched the jury carefully contemplate what the older man had said on the stand. He believed that Mr. Hickman had helped the case, just as he had promised he would.

The judge called a recess until 2:00 p.m. and people began shuffling out of the courtroom. Mr. Hickman left the stand. He had long ago escaped the violence of his marriage, but it had cost him all contact with his children. His trip to California had been an attempt to make up for all that, but it hadn't worked, at least as far as Ed was concerned. As he walked out of the courtroom, he tried to catch his son's eye. But as Richard Cantillon would recall years later, he failed. Ed walked out of the room with his gaze straight ahead. He never even glanced in his father's direction.

The defense attorneys were hesitant about their next witness – Eva Hickman, Ed's mother. After the lengthy testimony of William Hickman, they became concerned about Eva's fragile mental state. There was concern over whether she would make her son look more unstable, or less. Her unpredictable nature could hamper their efforts to help her son avoid the gallows, as much as it could help them.

Walsh and Cantillon met Eva Hickman for lunch and worked hard to make sure she understood the importance of her testimony. She seemed to understand and after spending most of the meal in silence, she finally began responding well to the lawyers' questions. She was not particularly well-spoken, but she was clear. She provided the information that they asked for and did not embellish anything. Cantillon noticed, though, that even when she seemed relaxed and comfortable with the attorneys, there was an underlying nervousness about her that made it seem as if she might burst into laughter or tears at any moment. The lawyers were hesitant about her, but they had no choice. They returned to the courthouse with Eva Hickman at 2:00 p.m., ready to continue with their client's defense.

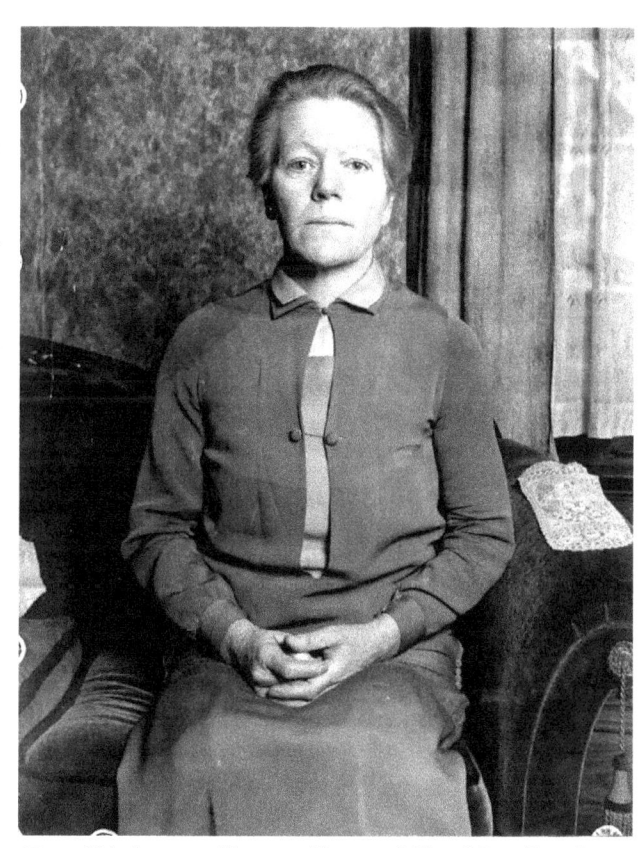

Eva Hickman, the mother of the "Fox," whose hereditary insanity was blamed for the heinous crime that he committed.

Everyone turned to look when Eva Hickman walked into the courtroom. Richard Cantillon led her into the room by the arm and they passed by the defense table, where her son was sitting with his head bowed. She put her hand on his shoulder and he looked up at her face. As their eyes met, something passed between them – a look, a moment, a knowing – but whatever it was, it was impossible for the reporters to describe. One woman who was seated nearby actually gasped, "Oh, my god!" The bailiff was so transfixed by the moment that he did not try to silence her. Hickman was startled by the woman's outburst and he quickly looked down again.

It was the judge who broke the tension. He banged his gavel," Will counsel direct his witness to the stand?"

Cantillon asked the judge to allow him to ask leading questions of the witness, a method not usually allowed in such cases. Eva Hickman, he knew, would have to be led to recall events that were necessary to the defense case. The prosecution objected, but the judge allowed it.

Eva was sworn in and took the stand. Her voice was weak and shaky and she had to be asked twice to speak up so that the jurors could hear her. Her testimony followed closely with what was recounted by William Hickman the previous day, although she offered even more details about her family's troubles. Jurors leaned toward her to listen as she recalled being a small child and carrying a lantern in the woods and fields as her father searched for her mother in the dark of night. Rebecca Buck's wailing cries served as the only guide to where the woman was hiding.

When it came to the state of her own mental health, however, Eva had no details. When Cantillon tried to lead her toward talking about her marriage to William Hickman and her reaction to him, emotionally and sexually, Eva continually muttered, "I can't recall."

With regards to Ed, she recalled his deep hatred of his father after William left the chaotic family life. As she spoke, her voice never raised higher than a loud whisper and the expression on her face never changed. She spoke of her son's gift for oration, his popularity in school, and his success as a teenager in academic and cultural events. She blamed his loss in the debate contest as the start of his decline into madness, which eventually led to his petty crimes. As she continued to talk about Ed, her voice began to quaver. She was almost unable to connect the son she once had to the monster that he had become.

After the forgery charge, Ed returned to Kansas City in disgrace. He was no longer the popular student and high school vice president. He was a thief, whose crimes had erased all his past accomplishments. Of course, his former friends, neighbors, and his mother had no idea that he had also committed two murders by this time. It was a secret that Hickman was able to keep until he was arrested for killing Marion Parker.

Eva ended her testimony with her recollection of Ed leaving home without saying goodbye and returning to California with the idea of coming up with $1,500 with which to enter college and become a minister. She did not hear from him again. Instead, she heard from a newsboy who was shouting headlines on a street corner that her son was wanted for the murder and dismemberment of a 12-year-old girl.

The prosecutors asked her no questions and Eva Hickman was allowed to leave the stand. She left the courtroom slowly, gently led by the arm out of the door from which she had entered. A reporter later wrote that it was obvious that a lifetime of suffering had etched itself on her face. She appeared to be drained, as if the questioning – and the horror of her son's acts – had taken away all of the strength that was left in her heart. The mother of Ed Hickman was suffering – the jurors could plainly see that. But it was not enough to make them forget how much more Marion Parker's mother was suffering because of the same brutal crime.

As the courtroom door closed behind Eva, all eyes in the room were on her – except for her son's. He was still staring down at the table.

The next part of the defense's case was the introduction of 85 pages of depositions into the record. And that was just the beginning. The defense counsel insisted on reading from 600 additional pages of material before calling another witness. The depositions were all an attempt to establish that insanity ran in Hickman's mother's family.

Walsh and Cantillon knew that such a plan was a risky one. Jurors are easily bored by such presentations, but Cantillon brought in his law partner, Frank Sievers, to do the reading. He had an exceptional voice and method of delivery that managed to keep the jury's attention.

It also didn't hurt that the depositions were rather disturbing.

One deposition was from Thomas Lewis, who was married to Eva Hickman's sister, Minnie. Lewis recalled that Otto Buck, the son of Eva and Minnie's brother, John, had suffered from fits since childhood. "He was foolish. He didn't have any mind. He talked and acted like a child.

He also described how Eva and Minnie's mother, Rebecca, would range in mood from deliriously happy to gloomy despair with alarming speed. Her husband stubbornly refused to admit that she might be insane. He believed that regular prayer would settle her into a state of normalcy. Of course, that never happened.

Lewis also noted that Eva Hickman's erratic behavior began when she started having children. She had started acting queer, he said, and talked foolishly. He ended his letter by stating, "I had a lot of confidence in

Edward. If that boy committed this awful crime, he has to be insane. There is no other way of accounting for it."

A deposition from Benjamin Harrison Bailey, brother-in-law of Otto Buck, Eva Hickman's brother, stated that Buck was "insane." Irvin Harris declared that grandma was "insane" when she died and Otto Buck was "crazy." Convinced that her neighbor's "had it in for her" and that her husband meant to poison her, Rebecca was known for running screaming through the fields of her Arkansas farm or weeping for hours in the corner of her barn. Paul Buck, Hickman's grandfather, was known to beat his livestock half to death during one of his frequent "mad fits" of rage.

Eva Hickman was deemed insane in a number of the depositions. Some of the letters came from doctors and others from friends, former neighbors, and relatives. Dr. W.D. Hunt of Poteau, Oklahoma, testified in his deposition that he had treated Eva Hickman from 1912 to 1920. He said that she had once tried to commit suicide and was later institutionalized. He concluded, "In my opinion, she is insane."

Sarah Stankard, a former neighbor, characterized Eva as "a little bit queer" and attested to Eva's attempted suicide. Artie Smith, Hickman's paternal aunt, told of Eva experiencing "dancing fits" that convinced her that she was "insane." Mae Forrester testified that Hickman's father had a reputation for "running around with women," which contributed to Eva's "nervous condition."

The terrible pain that had accompanied the delivery of Eva's first child reportedly left her with a terror of pregnancy and a deep abhorrence of sex. Persuaded by her religious zealot father that it was her duty to obey St. Paul's admonition – "Wives submit yourselves unto your husbands as you would unto the Lord"— she gave in to her husband's conjugal demands. Each of her subsequent pregnancies only drove her further into her "mania." When she found herself pregnant with Ed, she threatened to carve the baby out of her womb with a knife. His premature birth was particularly nightmarish after he almost died.

Eva gave birth to one more child, a daughter named Mary. Soon after she was born, Eva attempted suicide by swallowing carbolic acid and was committed to the state insane asylum. When she was released, she seemed much improved. Gradually, however, her madness returned. When her husband left for work in the morning, she would tell him that when he "came home, he would find the children all cut up and piled like cordwood in the middle of the floor." At night, sleeping in a room with all five children, he would awaken to find her standing at his bedside, a butcher's knife in her hand. He began barricading the door with a chair when they slept. Eventually, the situation became more than he could handle. In 1915, he abandoned his family and moved to New Mexico.

Ed was seven-years-old when his father left. Living in terrible poverty with a frighteningly unstable mother, Ed was taken under the wing of his fanatically religious grandfather. He accompanied the old man to frenzied, fire-and-brimstone tent meetings and the impressionable boy was soon infused with a burning zeal that, with his grandfather's encouragement, developed into a determination to become a minister.

However, his spiritual calling did not prevent him from indulging in extreme forms of cruelty, the depositions stated. Hickman was accused of capturing and torturing stray dogs and cats and on one occasion, he strangled the pet kitten of a neighbor girl who, even as an adult, vividly recalled the "apparent delight" that he derived from the act.

Ed was still a young boy when Eva, in an effort to stave off starvation, uprooted herself and the children from Arkansas and moved to Kansas City, Missouri. Her two oldest children soon found jobs and Ed devoted himself to his religious studies. By the time he entered high school, he was convinced that God meant for him to become "America's most influential clergyman."

From his freshmen through his junior years of school, he was an academic star, earning a straight-A average and excelling in every extracurricular activity that he attempted. During his senior year, though, he underwent the bizarre transformation from charming and ambitious student to a surly, paranoid loner.

And the reading went on and on.

Each of the depositions was read separately as a question-and-answer session, with all of the details included. Sievers's great speaking style kept the jurors interested, but caused some issues with the prosecution. They felt that his speaking style was editorializing the contents of the depositions, but the judge disagreed. And the reading continued – page after page. The defense was trying to show, once again, that Hickman was not at fault for what he had done. This time, it was his family that made him kill Marion.

At the conclusion of the day's "evidence," prosecution psychiatrists who had interviewed the defendant declared that the depositions that were read were meaningless and that none of them actually applied to the young man who was on trial. Unfortunately, though, the judge allowed them to continue and the depositions continued to be entered into evidence.

Otto F. Dubach, Hickman's high school principal, told of girls who had been acquaintances of the young man but said that he knew of no actual girlfriends in Hickman's past. A classmate stated that the defendant had never taken a girl to a dance, but preferred to "take girls away" from other boys and escort them home. Other instructors said that Hickman was a "very bright boy" in the upper 10 percent of his class with an excellent grade-point average. In various depositions, classmates and friends testified that Hickman seemed to "go through a change" between his junior and senior years. Some thought he was "insane," others that he was just "different."

Personally, I find the timeline of Hickman's "change" to be especially telling. I do not for a moment think that he was legally insane, but I do believe that he was greatly influenced by another kidnapping and murder that was in the news at that time. In fact, after he was captured in Oregon, he even quipped to reporters, "Do you think I'll be as famous as Leopold and Loeb?"

Described earlier, Richard Loeb and Nathan Leopold were two boys who were, like Hickman, of the belief they were of "superior intellect" and could commit the "perfect crime." As Hickman would eventually be after his "great crime," the two young men were captured and put on trial. After a lengthy trial, during which they were represented by the famed criminal attorney Clarence Darrow, they each received a sentence of life in prison, plus ninety-nine years for the kidnapping.

William Edward Hickman would not be so lucky.

After the depositions, court was adjourned until Monday. On Saturday, Walsh and Cantillon met with Hickman. On most days, their sullen client had very little to say, but on this days, the lawyers found him to be especially excited – just like he had been when he unleashed his detailed confession on them before the trial.

Hickman once again insisted on taking the stand. The attorneys were shocked. They felt they had already convinced Hickman that his testifying was a bad idea and could cripple his case. Hickman wanted to show how lucid he was, which was the exact opposite of what his counsel was trying to do. He was still seeing the trial as a sort of glorified "debate" – one side presenting something to convince the other side, using their skills to make

Hickman on his way into court from the jail. His attorney, Jerome Walsh, is on the left of the photograph.

a point. He didn't seem to understand that the prosecutors weren't trying to convince the defense team of anything. They were working to show the jury that Hickman was sane when he committed the murder. He carefully planned it and knew exactly what he was doing before, during, and after. Hickman wasn't insane – he was just plain evil. But no matter how long Walsh and Cantillon argued with him, Hickman insisted that he was going to testify.

Frustrated, they had their psychiatrist, Dr. A.L. Skoog, visit Hickman the following day. Cantillon recalled later that Skoog had a close understanding of Hickman's personality. After a visit from the doctor, during which Skoog and Hickman had a long discussion, Hickman told his lawyers that he was no longer interested in going on the stand.

But this would not be the last time that he would bring it up.

Court was again in session on Monday morning and the jurors heard from many more people from Hickman's past in the form of many more depositions. As Frank Sievers again presented each interview, the jury again heard how Hickman was described as a bright, likable young man who became withdrawn and difficult. One of the depositions came from his former employer at the market where Hickman had once worked, killing and dressing live chickens. He wrote, "He could not kill a chicken. He told me that he just did not have the heart to kill it. I just can't understand what happened to him. He must have gone completely crazy." Tragically, it was the skill that Hickman learned at the same poultry farm that enabled him to callously dismember Marion Parker.

Hickman sat silently and listened to the depositions that were offered by people who had once been his close friends. They could not believe that the boy they knew so well had been a monster all along. Hickman offered no reaction to any of it, at least until the testimony of Dr. Skoog was read into evidence the following day. Skoog took the stand and read, from his own notes, an interview that he had conducted with Hickman.

He began by asking Hickman if he was a Christian and Hickman stated that he was not. He said, "I have a power in me that is equal and which is more than God to anybody, but that nobody feels. They have something over them, and they are satisfied, and I am satisfied."

Skoog said that he understood that Hickman wanted to study for the ministry and Hickman replied that he did. He reiterated the fact that he felt there was a divine power, a providence, that was watching over him. It was superior to God and was especially for Hickman, no one else. Skoog went on to ask him about his statements about being "different." Did he think that meant he was crazy?

Hickman said that he didn't and added, "Crazy has a lot of different meanings. I have had lots of people call me crazy but I do not believe they meant it. Lots of times you say 'crazy' when you just mean queer or silly. But insanity is something I don't understand. I do not believe I am insane, but I am different from other people." He stressed that by "different" he did not mean in appearance. Dr. Skoog asked him if he thought that other people could tell he was different, just by looking at him, and Hickman replied that they might be able to once they knew his "secret."

Hickman told him, "After telling you my secret, you can understand."

"Is what you told me a sacred secret?" Dr. Skoog asked.

"Yes, sir, I seldom tell anybody."

Skoog asked him if he was directed by someone to keep this secret and Hickman shrugged. "I can tell you," he said. "I told my mother of it. I told my friend, Don Johnstone. I told Mr. Cantillon and Dr. Shelton because they must know to understand me. They are helping me. I told Mr. Moise, a reporter who comes to visit me; he is writing a story about me. I never like to disclose my complete views on it; that is, in trying to explain it, I just haven't words to give the exact idea of it. It talks to me and suggests things. I hear it; I have seen it. Beyond any doubt, it really exists. It has been known to me for a long time. I do not try to overcome this power. It is far greater than I am. I am humble, passive, and obedient to it. It is something I should not try to understand."

Dr. Skoog asked him to explain further and Hickman replied that he felt the "power" take him over and with its aid, he would become a great man. If the power told him to do something, he did it. He said that he believed that it planned everything in his life. He told Skoog, "All human beings, no matter how smart they are, have only a shade of conception of the universe. But the power knows it all. It is supreme greatness. I used the name providence, but that does not exactly describe it.

"Do you know of anyone else with whom your providence communicates?" Skoog asked him.

"It has not been revealed to anyone else, not even Christ."

"You say providence talks to you; how does it sound?"

"It is soft, but powerful. When it is speaking, I cannot move. Chills run down my spine."

"You have seen pictures of God in white flowing robes. I presume your providence appears much like God," Skoog suggested.

Hickman shook his head. "No, my providence has fiery eyes; they seem to burn a hole in me. It does not wear robes. It wears a white suit, shirt, tie, and shoes. It looks so strong, it frightens me."

"But why should you be afraid?" Skoog asked. "It is your benefactor."

"There are things, I told you, I just don't understand."

"But your power won't reveal these things to you?"

"I think it will be told to me, when it wants me to know," Hickman stated. "Not until then."

When asked to explain what was in his statement, Dr. Skoog concluded that Hickman's visions of "providence" stemmed from a grandiose delusion that was common in paranoid schizophrenics.

Dr. Skoog left the stand and court was adjourned for the day. As the lawyers were packing up their briefcases, a deputy sheriff approached Walsh and Cantillon and told them that Hickman was asking to see them right away.

They met with Hickman about an hour later. He was furious, pacing his cell like a caged animal, with his eyes wide and shiny. This was not stress about the case, this was a burning anger that Cantillon later wrote could be "dangerous." The lawyers were not in danger; there were guards everywhere but they knew that Hickman's agitated state had to be handled. After a few seconds of watching Hickman pace, Cantillon finally asked him what was wrong.

Hickman screamed at them, "I thought those doctors were my friends! I am going to take the stand and tell the jury they are telling a pack of lies!"

Hickman's "secret" was not only in the court record, but would make its way into the newspapers. Hickman was livid. Something that he considered private, special, even sacred, had been revealed as the delusional ravings of a madman. Hickman wanted to plead insanity to save himself from the gallows, but he didn't want anyone to think he was actually crazy.

"Don't you believe me?" he asked his lawyers. Hickman then fell to his knees and began to sob.

Cantillon managed to calm him down and assured him that the testimony would help with the case. It took a few minutes, but Hickman eventually stopped crying and regained his composure. He said that he was willing to let his attorneys do what they thought was best for the case. His demeanor changed and he became the stiff and sullen defendant that they were used to again.

Cantillon would later write that this was the last time he ever saw Hickman cry.

Dr. Skoog's testimony continued the following day. He had more to read about what Hickman had revealed to him during their sessions. The attorneys wanted to use Hickman's own words to convince the jury of his insanity – they just didn't want him on the stand testifying.

During the session, Dr. Skoog had asked Hickman about his feelings for Marion. He offered some unusual comments. "I think she was actually born and lived for this thing," he said. "It is true she may not then have known about it, but she was prepared and brought into this world for this very thing."

Skoog asked him if she knew about it now, and Hickman answered that he believed that she did, but she was not angry with him. "I killed her. Yes, I murdered her," he explained, "but I don't think I took her life away."

When Skoog asked him to explain, Hickman stated that she was predestined to be his victim. He told Dr. Skoog, "She told me that a week before the kidnapping she dreamt that a strange man came to the school and took her away. She told me that she had several dreams about this before. She said her mother always warned her about getting in an automobile with a strange man. She told me that she never thought it would be so bad to be kidnapped. She said that in her daydreams at her desk in school she had also imagined this. I felt this was a positive manifestation of this power that I have been trying to describe as having influence over me. It was all prearranged."

While few in the courtroom seemed bothered by Hickman's statements about divine providence convincing him of the need to murder and butcher a little girl, everyone became very uncomfortable when the testimony turned to sex. There had been no evidence that Marion had been sexually assaulted, and yet, rumors suggested that if Hickman was sick enough to kill and dismember her, perhaps he had sexually assaulted her, too.

Hickman was adamant about the fact that he did not. He never took advantage of Marion in that manner and, in fact, never even thought of doing so. He was a strange young man, but apparently had not been motivated by sex. Dr. Skoog had asked him about his past sexual encounters with girls, which were limited, and he was asked to talk about how often he masturbated. There was a rustle of embarrassment throughout the courtroom during this part of the testimony, but Skoog's questions were important to the case – and to the public. No matter what terrible things had happened to Marion, it was made quite clear that nothing of a sexual nature had occurred. For that much, Americans could breathe a sigh of relief.

Throughout all of this, Hickman sat silently, his head down, listening to Dr. Skoog detail their intimate conversation. The jury listened closely, knowing that with each day that passed, they were closer to being called upon to decide the defendant's fate.

Hickman was becoming impatient with the trial. He had resigned himself to hanging for Marion's murder and often told Walsh and Cantillon that he just wanted to get it over with. They encouraged him by saying that they believed he could be saved from the gallows. This quieted Hickman down, for a little while anyway.

The nation was probably more impatient than Hickman. As the trial was reported in the newspapers, the public anxiously awaited its outcome. Letters flooded into the courthouse and the jail, demanding that California "give this monster the execution he deserves." The public didn't care about his alleged insanity. Hickman was a fiend who had killed an innocent girl. Marion Parker had become a symbol of every American child who might possibly be victim to the same kind of danger. Parents watched their own children a little closer and warned them of the danger of strangers in a way they never had to do before. Attendance in schools dropped sharply for a time. Many seemed to feel that Hickman's execution would serve as a warning to any potential child killers that such things would not be tolerated in America. Hickman wasn't going to get away with it, like Leopold and Loeb had.

While his attorneys were working to save him from the gallows, as Clarence Darrow had done for his infamous clients in Chicago, in the eyes of the public, William Edward Hickman was a merciless killer who deserved to be hanged.

Of course, a jury is nothing more than 12 people chosen from the public.

The public was impatient, but they would not have to wait much longer. The time had come for closing statements in the trial, and both Walsh and Cantillon felt that it was crucial for the defense team to open and close the arguments. They felt that since they had carried the burden of proof, they should be the last side to be heard.

The judge, however, disagreed.

The defense lawyers were crestfallen. They had defended a man who had killed and dismembered a little girl. The public had been thirsting for his blood since first reading about Marion's ordeal in the newspapers. The first and last words in his trial would be spoken by the prosecution. It was an omen of bad things ahead.

Forrest Murray of the prosecution made the first closing statement. Murray was an eloquent man and his passionate delivery enhanced every word. The jury and the spectators sat quietly, taking in everything he said. No one in the courtroom seemed to take a breath. Even Richard Cantillon would later write about Murray's piercing presentation, the power of his speech, and the way he communicated with the jury. He knew that it was a difficult act to have to follow.

Murray walked to the podium and addressed the court:

This has been a long and arduous trial surcharged with disturbing emotion. It is nearly over. Very soon you jurors who attentively listened to the evidence will retire to deliberate upon a verdict. There is but a single issue of fact to be determined by you. It is this: did the defendant appreciate the character of his act and know it was wrong? That is the legal standard of responsibility. You dare not presume yourself wiser than the law. Judge Trabucco will charge that if William Edward Hickman knew right from wrong in relation to the killing of Marion Parker, your verdict shall be that the defendant is sane.

During the trial I have made judicious observation which I trust will be of assistance to you in reaching your decision that the defendant did know right from wrong. On July 15, 1927, in this identical courtroom, the same defendant stood before the court accused of forgery. The perpetrator of the crime had for his purpose the taking of another's money through fraud. Deliberate scheming and specific criminal intent accomplish forgery. The defendant, when caught, pleaded guilty, thus admitting that he knew the wrongfulness of that criminal act.

Five months later, the defendant is before this court accused of kidnapping-murder. The perpetrator of his crime had for his purpose the taking of another's money through extortion. The crime here was also accomplished by deliberate scheming and specific criminal intent. The defendant, caught red-handed, pleads not guilty by reason of insanity, thus asserting that he did not know the wrongfulness of that murderous act.

Ladies and gentlemen, it is the difference in punishment for the crimes of forgery and murder that prompted the plea of not guilty by reason of insanity; it is not the difference in the defendant's mental condition in July and December.

Their defense of insanity rests on the premise that the defendant was under a delusion that he was directed and protected by a supernatural power in his killing of Marion Parker and did not know right from wrong. They illogically claim that the atrociousness of the crime proves this. I ask you to apply the touchstone of reason to the evidence to determine whether this premise is true or false. Always keep in mind that a man's knowledge of right from wrong can best be interpreted by his actions.

Why did Hickman assume false names – the name Evans when he rented an apartment upon his arrival here from Kansas City; the name Cooper when he abducted the child from school; the name Palmer at a San Francisco hotel when in flight from California; the name Peck when the Pendleton police arrested him? He did this to avoid detection. Why? Because he knew he was guilty of premediated kidnapping and murder and feared the consequences.

Why did he repeatedly warn Mr. Parker in letters and telephone calls not to contact the police? It was because he knew he was guilty of a capital crime and, if apprehended, would be punished accordingly.

When Hickman exchanged the mutilated remains of the child with her father for the gold certificates, why did he carry an automatic, bend his license plates, and mask his face? It transcends all reason to say he did not know full well the criminality of that grisly transaction.

Why did Hickman abandon his Chrysler in which he delivered the child's body; at gun point take a Hudson from its owner; and then flee the state of California? There is but one reason for his actions: his consciousness of guilt compelled him to become a fugitive from the justice he knew he deserved.

All the matters embodied in these four questions conclusively imply the defendant's knowledge of the wrongfulness of his acts. For you jurors to find otherwise would be not only a fallacy, but folly. Ladies and gentlemen, you are the triers of fact. The sole issue for your considerations was whether or not Hickman knew his killing of Marion Parker was wrong. If he did, he is responsible to the law. There is but one verdict the evidence can support: the defendant is sane. His acts were cruel, premeditated deliberate acts of a callous criminal. His was not the confused, purposeless act of the mentally sick. He committed this terrible crime to satisfy his greed for money. Hickman did not rely on a special providence to protect him as he here represents. He relied upon criminal cunning and a fast shooting automatic pistol.

To me the defense of insanity is a sham. It is as ridiculous as if the defendant had pleaded self-defense. The bucket just doesn't hold water. I turn this case over to you. You have a most solemn duty to perform.

You must not fail.

Murray's speech stunned everyone in the room. He had carefully presented all of the holes in the defense's argument, offering specific examples to back up his belief that Hickman was sane, in charge of his faculties, and knew exactly what he was doing when he killed and dismembered Marion Parker. His indication of proof was compelling, and it played well with the public, who wanted Hickman to die for what he had done.

Walsh and Cantillon listened as closely as the jury did. Their statement had already been prepared, but they jotted down hurried notes to supplement the statement that had been written with points with which to counter Murray's closing. The judge allowed them a 10-minute recess while they huddled together. Walsh would be speaking first and then Cantillon would follow him. Then, the prosecution would get the final word. After that, it was up to the jury to bring in their verdict.

After time had passed, the judge gave Walsh permission to proceed:

The Prosecutor, Murray, has selected a little pile of triviality from the mass of weighty evidence, and by inlaying these small pieces of various colored circumstances, he has fabricated a mosaic with which he hopes to dazzle your judgment. These special circumstances can be summed up as the defendant's concealment of his identity, his avoidance of detection, the use of deadly weapons, and the flight from this state. Murray has taken these incidents out of context to prove William Edward Hickman sane. When we properly consider Murray's incidents along with the major acts preceding and following, they are but tints on the powerful portrait of schizophrenia.

If you carefully consider my worthy opponent's argument, you will find that it is composed of three propositions. First, that the defendant's fear of consequences proves that he knew right from wrong in relation to the act of killing. Second, that greed for money motivated the defendant to kill Marion Parker. Third, that you should except as true the opinions given by medical witnesses produced by the prosecutors. If you will, as Mr. Murray requested, and here I insist, apply the touchstone of reason, I am certain that the evidence to which I will draw your attention will contradict each and all of the prosecutions contentions.

We will consider the first proposition that the defendant feared the consequences of his act. If the preponderance of the evidence establishes that the defendant could not entertain a fear of consequence, this theory contended for by the prosecutor is refuted. What is fear? It is a strong emotion caused by an awareness of danger.

On the subject of fear, the evidence establishes that the defendant repeatedly precipitated situations fraught with danger. Can he be said to have feared the danger he deliberately created? When the defendant openly kidnapped Marian Parker from a public school, he toyed with danger. He courted danger on Friday night when, with the kidnapped child in his automobile, he rode in the police procession to Tenth and Gramercy. He defied danger and death when he delivered the child's mutilated body to her father, whom he had every reason to believe would be accompanied by the police. He exhibited absolute disregard for danger when, knowing an intensive police search for him was in full swing, he went to the busy intersection of Western and Hollywood and robbed Fred Peck of his automobile.

The insanity of this boy is made manifest by his inability to react normally to the awareness of danger. His emotional functioning which produces fear is peculiarly paralyzed by schizophrenia, a dread disease.

Warnings, weapons, concealment of identity, and flight are all in the nature of innate impulses and our circumstances far subordinate to the major facts of this case. These incidents do not establish the sanity of one who strangled a child, mutilated her body, wired open the eyes, and rouged the face, and delivered it to her father for $1,500. Particularly is this so when it develops that his money is wanted for a religious education. The major facts as proof of insanity far outweigh the minor circumstances on which Mr. Murray predicates his sanity claim. Your findings on this issue in this case must be made on the overall picture, not just isolated incidents as Mr. Murray urges.

Mr. Murray further asserts that the defendant was motivated to kill Marion Parker by his greed for money. Apparently, the prosecution and the defense are not too far apart in their respective appraisals of this case. Greed is a desire for money that exceeds the limit of reason. As counsel for the defendant, I too agree that the defendant's inordinate money acquisitiveness exceeded the limit of reason. Yes! It exceeded the limit of rationality. It spawns directly from his insane delusion; it is stark madness. In the Kansas City depositions, prosecutor Castillo asked Mr. Laughlin, the assistant high school principal, if it would change his opinion that Hickman was insane if he knew his motive for killing Marion Parker was to obtain $1,500 to defray his expenses at Park College. Mr. Laughlin logically analyzes the defendant's morbid self-contradictory behavior. Hickman's purpose was to become an evangelist and reconcile sinful man to God through Christ, so in furtherance of this purpose, he had killed God's greatest treasure, a guileless little girl. "No, Mr. Costello," Laughlin replied, "it would not change my opinion; it would make me feel more than ever that the boy is insane because Park College is an ecclesiastical institution."

Mr. Murray on the proposition of greed tells but half the story. The defendant was indeed possessed of a desire for $1,500 that exceeded the limits of reason. But Mr. Murray doesn't tell you that this obsessive desire stemmed from an insane delusion that Almighty Providence directed the defendant to acquire this money for schooling to become a minister of Christ. This is the whole story. On the greed issue the facts in their entirety preponderated in favor of the defense.

Each of you jurors took a sacred oath that you could and would eradicate bias and prejudice from your thinking and return a verdict based solely upon the evidence in this case. The evidence overwhelmingly establishes that this boy suffers from mental disease. It clearly shows that he conjured, through six fantasy, a false God. His disease-twisted thinking affected transference of the obedience due the Almighty to his morbid Providence. At this Providence's command, he killed Marion Parker. In this fevered mental state, he could not know right from wrong.

"Thou shall not kill" is an admonition not alone from the sovereign state, but from Almighty God. It applies with equal force to all competent, responsible mortals. This may be the only time in your lives when you come face-to-face with this divine injunction. If one of you sitting in the jury box should in the deliberations join in a verdict adverse to this boy, motivated by prejudice or to gain public approbation, you will have violated the commandment of God, "thou shout not kill." And that one will be called upon to pay the awful penalty for perfidy and murder in God's chosen manner, in God's chosen time.

Walsh walked slowly back to his seat at the defense table. During his statement, he had paused dramatically several times, drinking from a water glass, and looking disturbed by the speech he had to deliver. It boiled down to the fact that he stated that the jurors would be murderers – just like his client – according to the judgment of God if they put Hickman to death. Murray had used the law to drive his point home with the jury, while Walsh had used morals, superstitions, and fear. No one could be sure how the jury would react to either.

One of the most effective parts of Walsh's closing was the way that he pointed out Hickman's lack of fear or nervousness when he committed Marion's murder. This was, Walsh suggested, caused by his lack of sanity. The jurors could see this demonstrated right before their eyes. Hickman was on trial for his life, but one would never know it. He sat quietly at the defense table, his head down, showing no emotion whatsoever. Walsh said that he had been unaware of the danger he was in with the kidnapping and eventual murder – and the jury could clearly see this in the courtroom. Hickman seemed disinterested in the fact that a vote either way from the jury meant life of death for him.

A newspaper photograph of Richard Cantillon from another case around the time of the Hickman trial. He is the younger man, standing in the center of the photograph.

After a two-hour adjournment for lunch, court was called back to order. It was now Richard Cantillon's turn to speak for the defense. He had skipped lunch and had spent two hours in the law library putting the finishing touches on his presentation. District Attorney Asa Keyes would have the last word for the prosecution, so Cantillon knew that his closing for the jury had to be even more forceful than Walsh's had been, or Hickman would surely hang.

When he took center stage in the courtroom, Cantillon thanked the judge, the jury, and paid his respects to the prosecution. He then began his statement – the last words from the defense that the jury would hear:

When you were questioned at the time you were first called into the jury box, all of you stated that you entertained a preconceived opinion. I am not insensible to the nature of that opinion. The panic in terror of that awful Saturday night incensed revulsion and revenge. Each of you swore that you would vanish from your mind your preconceived opinion and base your verdict solely on the evidence. It was upon this solemn assurance that you qualified to act as a trier of the facts in the case at bar. As sworn jurors, you became a component of the judiciary. No longer can you entertain belief of sanity or insanity upon rumor and report. Your decision must be based only upon judicial evidence. That is, the sworn testimony given by the witnesses, the sworn testimony read from the depositions, and the exhibits introduced during the trial. To consider a rumor or report secretly or openly in your deliberations would be to violate your sacred oath.

As trial jurors, it is your duty to except and apply the law as given to you by the trial judge. The court will charge you that under law an insane man is incapable of committing murder or any other crime. This is a cardinal principle of criminal justice. You as jurors dare not presume yourselves wiser than the law. The question as to whether William Edward Hickman is sane or insane is not one of medical science or legal Definition. It is a question to be answered by your common sense. An impartial consideration of the evidence will satisfy you that it is far more probable the boy is insane.

We must consider the nature of insanity. It is a disorder of the thought processes of the mind. The mind is capable of definition only as it relates to its functions. It thinks, it feels, it wills, and thereby governs all human behavior. The psychiatrist call these functions intellection, emotion, and volition. The brain, the organ of the mind, is a mass of nerve tissue contained within the cranium. The special function of this organ has been said, by analogy, to secrete thoughts as the liver secretes bile. The brain is subject to the ravages of disease as are the lungs, the heart, and all other bodily organs. When this occurs, the interconnected mental functions become deranged and the thoughts fantastic, resulting in bizarre behavior that is often dangerous.

Our defense is that William Edward Hickman is sick, desperately sick. He suffers from a mental disease called schizophrenia. The doctors for the prosecution and the defense agree that the predisposing cause of schizophrenia is heredity. They agreed that an unstable environment and puberty are the precipitating factors; that a personality change and fixed, systematized, dominant delusion accompanies the disease. Here all agreement among these professional men ends. The doctors for the defense claim this boy is pathetically insane, and that all essential symptoms for a diagnosis of schizophrenia are present. The doctors for the prosecution say he is sane and his behavior normal. They cannot find in all his frightful evidence a single symptom of mental derangement. Between this conflicting evidence it is your duty to exercise commonsense and determine wherein the truth lies.

To aid in your deliberations, it is my purpose to focus your attention on evidence which clearly proves, to the point of demonstration, that the defendant is insane. On the subject of the defendant's heredity and environment during his formative years, sixteen witnesses from the Ozarks testified. They were immediate family, relatives, neighbors, attending physicians, and a registered nurse. The prosecution produced nothing contradictory, although it commands the financial and legal resources of the state of California and has the cooperation of authorities everywhere.

The witnesses painted a picture of an old woman tortured by paranoid delusions – Becky Buck, the crazy grandmother of the defendant.

Witnesses also described a Bible-reading old man, a religious camp meeting revivalist who, when triggered by the slightest incident, would fly into rages -- Paul Buck, the psycho-neurotic grandfather of the defendant.

Graphically these witnesses then etched a poor "slobbering, wallowing" epileptic imbecile, who foolishly followed his wife while she worked in the fields for their subsistence. This was Otto Buck, the defendant's first cousin

These witnesses further drew a word picture of a mother standing in a dim light over her sleeping children, butcher knife upraised; a wife silently moving in night-darkened hallways, hatchet in hand, bent on killing her husband; a woman frustrated in her homicidal efforts drinking a caustic acid in an attempt at self-destruction; a woman committed to the state asylum as dangerously insane. This was Eva Hickman, the schizophrenic mother of the defendant.

Interwoven in this proof of insane heredity is the evidence of the precipitating factor of an unstable environment. The nocturnal screams and struggles, his demented mother's attempts at homicide and suicide, the frenzied religious exorcisms to which the grandfather subjected the child, sudden desertion by his father, the obsessive hate, privation, and hunger were the soil where the seed flourished.

The power of procreation in the male begins at puberty. He is then between twelve to fourteen years of age. Puberty is accompanied by drastic bodily changes which continue into the maturity of his twenties. To a boy predisposed to schizophrenia, this is a critical period, as schizophrenia is the disease of adolescence. Medical experts are becoming convinced from the research that it is the alteration in the chemistry of the body, brought on by the glandular changes that results in the pubescent shock, which is so devastating to the adolescent, predisposed to schizophrenia.

The facts of this case amply establish the drastic change in the personality of William Edward Hickman which accompanied his pubescent bodily changes. The doctors consider this change an essential symptom of schizophrenia. Through witnesses who knew him best in his high school days, fellow students, teachers, adult friends, and employers, we show that this boy possessed all the sterling qualities that we look for in an outstanding man.

With great current courage he overcame the almost insurmountable obstacles that poverty places in the path of the poor. Although compelled to work for a living, his intellectual attainment surpassed those of any of the 3,000 students in Central High School. He participated in all oratorical contests, winning or placing highly in these endeavors. His fellow students elected him Vice President of their senior class. He became President of the school chapter of the National Honor Society. He was deeply religious; his goal was the ministry. He was sensitive to suffering, sacrificing his limited recreation time to visit a friend who was in his last illness. This tender-hearted boy could not bring himself to kill a chicken.

Within a period of months, we find him in this courtroom on trial for murder. What caused the terrible change in this boy's personality? The answer is disease. You've seen a strong body rendered helplessly crippled by polio. Here you see a strong mind rendered hopelessly maniacal by schizophrenia.

Now let me take up the matter of the defendant's delusion. This is, by its very nature, the difficult symptom to prove because it is subjective; that is, perceptible only to the deranged one. The defendant, in his written statement made for District Attorney Keyes en route from Oregon to Los Angeles, referred to this delusion. I will read a portion of that writing from the exhibit in evidence.

The fact that I, a young man, was willing to commit murder to secure expenses through college, and especially a church school, helps to explain me. This was my great motive. I cannot understand it myself. In the murder of Marion Parker, I could not

realize this terrible guilt. I felt Providence was guiding and directing me in this.

District Attorney Keyes signed this written statement as a witness. I cannot say what Mr. Keyes's reaction was to the defendant's reference to his Providence. But this I know; the district attorney had a brain surgeon, Dr. C, waiting for Hickman's arrival at the county jail. Why? In the jury room in your deliberations, your jurors ask and answer that question.

In every psychiatric examination of the boy thereafter, he repeated his relationship to this strange deity he called Providence. Did he believe this? The matter, as I will call to your attention, will convince you that he did. Religion is recognition on the part of man of a controlling superhuman power entitled to obedience. The dominant influence in this boy's childhood with his grandfather, Paul Buck, who followed the biblical proverb, "Train up your child in the way he should go and when he is old he will not depart from it." In his zealotry, the grandfather exposed his grandchild to frenzied religious exorcisms, placing further strain on this child's predisposed emotional instability.

When mental disease distorted the boys thinking processes, he became in capable of attaining his life's goal. He withdrew into a world of sick imagination. Here his burning ambition was more than satisfied; he became the sole earthly agent of the Super God and the only object of his bounty. In return he permuted the absolute obedience due his Maker to this false Super God. Out of the limbo of his subconscious mind, surcharged with severe repressions of this awful childhood, homicide and mutilation ideated. These repressions stemmed from the conduct and threats of his demented mother, as testified by his father. When his Super God commanded him to take a human life, this boy was powerless to disobey. Under such delusive influence, he strangled Marion Parker.

When Hickman hung that little dead body head down over the bathtub drain and cut the throat with a kitchen knife, when he severed the arms and legs, when he disemboweled the child, when he dressed what remained of her in her school clothes, when he rouged her face, applied lipstick to that little dead mouth, and wired open the eyes, he was not malingering – he was completely mad.

Under the enlightened influence of civilization, a refined law decrees the non-responsibility of one suffering from insanity. This is the charity of the law. Regardless of public excitement and vindictiveness, this is the law of our land and upon the strength and courage of you jurors, its just *application rests. These are all the bizarre acts of a diseased mind. They have caused horror and loathing, but it is this boy's mental condition upon what your verdict must be grounded, not on your emotional reaction to his irrational behavior.*

Cantillon concluded his lengthy statement. His mouth was dry and his face flushed. He and Walsh had now done everything they could do for their client. The jurors, to their credit with all the noise the case had caused in the newspapers, listened closely to them.

Years later, in the book that he wrote about the case, Cantillon recalled being satisfied with his closing argument. He had logically broken down the defense presented in the trial, discussing Hickman's history. One of the most powerful lines – "You have seen a strong body rendered helplessly crippled by polio. Here you see a strong mind rendered hopelessly maniacal by schizophrenia." – was something that the jury could easily understand. A polio victim's body turned against them and Hickman, he had argued, was victim of his mind.

District Attorney Asa Keyes would provide the conclusion to the trial. He had been involved in the case since the beginning and had ridden the train with Hickman from Oregon to California. He had been witness to Hickman's original confession and was part of the conversation between Hickman and Detective Herman Cline about the gruesome parts of the story that Cline said would "hang Hickman."

The most chilling parts of the case were not public at the time. The most graphic details were not yet allowed in the mainstream press. The public knew the basic facts of the murder, but not all the gory details. But the jury had heard everything – and they were the ones who would decide Hickman's fate.

Cantillon and Walsh had contended that Hickman's horrible act was the result of a sick mind. The jury would decide if he was indeed insane at the time he committed the murder or whether he was acting out of evil, stemming from malice and greed.

But first, they had to hear from the district attorney and Asa Keyes was an experienced prosecutor, and a clever man with a sardonic wit that he often injected into his statements to excite juries. It was always effective, especially when dealing with the prejudices of a jury against a brutal child killer like Hickman.

Keyes stepped out into the center of the room and addressed the jury. He waved an arm toward the defense table as he began to speak, noting first, "These young men who have undertaken the defense of this defendant have done a masterful job," he said. "I am pleased."

Keyes turned back toward the jury when he spoke next. "No one witnessing this trial can ever say that the defendant has not had the full measure of his rights. This establishes confidence and respect for our judicial system. For if people did not have the confidence and respect for the jury system and know that justice will be done, Hickman would not be here today. If people were not civilized, the mob would take this man from the law officers. I would have been in the forefront of the mob trying to put a noose around the neck of the defendant if I did not honor the law."

The district attorney paused and looked back over at Hickman. He stared at him for a moment and Hickman, sitting stoically at the defense table with this head down, looked up at him for a moment. There was no expression on his face.

Keys shook his head and spoke, "I'm not going to get into the horrible details of this crime. We have been criticized for giving this man a trial at all by certain people…"

Suddenly, Walsh and Cantillon both sprang from their seats, exploding in loud objections. Keyes's words were deemed prejudicial by the judge, and the jurors were asked not to consider Keyes's remarks as evidence. But Keyes knew exactly what he was doing – and he knew the jury would not forget what he said.

He continued with his closing statement:

I'm going to be fair to Hickman although I loathe the ground he walks on.

Do you know that it is the duty of the D.A. prosecuting the defendant to guard his rights and see that no right is violated? It is not the duty of the D.A. to inflame the juries mind against the defendant.

Hickman started his insanity dodge in the Pendleton jail and he's just as smart now as when he won second place in the oratorical contest in Kansas City. He knew the only way to attempt to dodge the gallows was by insanity, and he was smart enough to try and fool the jury. Dr. Skoog submitted the defendant to asinine tests that I never heard of before.

Do you think this man who committed this crime when he took the body to the father and grabbed the $1,500, armed with a loaded gun, believed he was protected by divine Providence to give a great message to the world? He did not tell the father, "I committed this crime so the eyes of the world would be directed to me." He acted like every other criminal. At the point of a gun, he took the $1500 and drove away in his stolen automobile, and made the detection impossible. He did not say, "I want the eyes of the world on me for the commission of this crime." He did not want the eyes of the world upon him; he sought cover so not a single eye on the face of the earth could see him. Old Doc Skoog, the country gentleman from Kansas City, swallowed what Hickman told him hook, line, and sinker.

Most of the crimes committed in the United States are committed by young men between the ages of fifteen and twenty-three. Whether a young man goes straight or crooked is not shaped by divine Providence, but by himself. Hickman is not insane; he is bad, rotten to the core. He committed grave crimes after he left high school and the parental rough. He did not want to apply himself to work; he wanted to make money the easy way.

Don't you see, ladies and gentlemen of the jury, don't you gather from what these doctors tell you that this demential praecox, paranoid form, that a man who is really afflicted with that, then a man who really has it, then a man who really commits a crime guided and influenced and directed by his insane delusion tells you all? He is proud of it; his mind is full of it; he can't think of anything else. You know that is a fact. They tell you so. That has been their observation; that has been my observation. Don't you believe that if this defendant had really and truly had, at the time or has now, dementia praecox of the paranoid type, that when he was arrested there in Pendleton, and old man Gurdane, the gentleman who covered him with a gun and put him under arrest, first talked to him, what would have been the most natural thing for that man to have uttered when asked his name? They say he is full of grandiose ideas, exalted ego. He said his name was Peck. Was there any exalted ego in that statement? Was there anything in those actions to lead you to believe that he was actuated or had any grandiose ideas?

A sane man would do just exactly as the Fox did on that occasion. If you had been insane, ladies and gentlemen, if he had dementia praecox, paranoid form, with the delusion which these doctors say he had, he would have said, "Mr. Chief of Police, my name is William Edward Hickman. I killed the Parker girl, but I did it because I was guided by divine Providence. I did it because I want my name to be blazoned across the portals of mankind down through the ages, to go as the perpetrator of the most atrocious crime that has ever been committed in the United States. I am proud of it. I have been directed by divine Providence, by my Supreme Being, to do it." He did not say that, did he? No, he did not, and he never mentioned anything about a divine Providence to any single living soul, or never claimed that he was guided by it until he had time to figure out in the Pendleton jail what his defense of this matter was going to be.

I think he was a monster without a soul, without conscience, without a heart. When he committed forgery, he made no claim that divine Providence guided him. He printed his ransom notes to disguise his hand writing so his identity would be kept in the dark. If he thought he was guided by Providence, why would he be trying to conceal his identity? Hickman did not believe in God. He who believes he is above the Savior of mankind penned a note to the poor suffering father informing him to ask God for aid.

A lot of people say they can't understand how Hickman could've committed such a crime if he was in his right mind. He is a criminal; he is a bad man; he is a man without a soul, without a conscience, without a heart. He is not an All-American boy; he is an American criminal who, with the aid of your verdict, the state of California will purge from its borders. I want this jury to show the people of the United States what the far western state of California says to people who commit crimes like this within its borders.

There have been mobs formed in the city of Los Angeles to deal with this man. All the way from Pendleton until we got to Los Angeles, there were mobs at every station. I stood behind this boy to see that no mob violence overtook him; he's entitled to that. If it were to come to pass through any effort of mine that the law of the state of California was to become a mockery, it would be better for me if I had never been born.

I'm going to submit this matter to you at this time with the hope that it does not go out to the Atlantic seaboard and the countries of the world that the state of California is not able to adequately cope with a criminal, because a criminal the man is; he is not insane.

With that final statement, Keyes concluded his closing statement, and the trial of William Edward Hickman, for the murder of Marion Parker, was over. After more than a month of newspaper stories that had informed the public of the kidnapping, ransom, murder, pursuit, and eventual capture of the criminal, the trial was completed in just 15 days.

It was now time for the jury to decide Hickman's fate.

Before they left the box for the jury room, the judge carefully explained the definition of insanity and how it applied to the law and the Hickman case. He explained, "You are to determine what the condition of the defendant's mind was at the precise time of the commission of the acts charged in the indictment. Its condition before or afterward is only to be considered by you for the purpose of throwing light upon its state of the commission of said acts."

The jury retired to try and reach a verdict at 2:20 p.m. They returned to the courtroom just 43 minutes later. It had taken less than an hour for the eight men and four women to determine the fate of William Edward Hickman. The vote had been unanimous.

Hickman was sane.

He knew what he was doing when he murdered and dismembered Marion Parker. He understood right from wrong and he comprehended the gravity of his actions. He was legally responsible for his crimes.

DEATH FOR THE "FOX"

The next day, newspapers across the country triumphantly announced that the jury had found Hickman to be sane. He was responsible for the murder of little Marion Parker. The case that District Attorney Keyes referred to as "the most atrocious crime ever committed in the United States" and that had become a part of popular culture by finding its way in newspaper editorial cartoons, poems, and even the repertoire of murder ballad folk sings, had ended with a verdict that condemned the killer to death.

Editorials speculated about Hickman's ultimate fate. Death by hanging was the standard in California in 1928, held over from frontier days that were not too far in the past. Would Hickman be hanged? Or would he end up spending the rest of his life in prison after all? The public eagerly snatched up newspapers and discussed it among themselves. People across the country had been talking about the case as it unfolded and everyone had an opinion. The general consensus seemed to be that Hickman should hang. His guilty verdict was celebrated by some, with reports of parties being thrown in honor of Marion Parker and condemning Hickman as a convicted killer who would get the ending that he deserved.

An emotionally exhausted Perry Parker spoke only briefly to the press. He was glad that the trial was over and that the jury realized that it was his daughter, not Hickman, who was the victim in the case. He and his family just wanted to get on with their lives and do their best to cherish the memory of the daughter who was taken from them too soon. It was something that he continued to say to the press until the case faded from the headlines and reporters finally left the Parker family alone to finally get on with their lives.

Hickman had sat quietly, emotionless, in the courtroom as the verdict had been read. It was the same manner in which he had listened to his family history and his various quirks announced to the court. The facts, the unflattering testimonies, and the statements by the defense and the prosecutors had painted him as either a monster or an insane person. He even had to hear what he told the doctor about how often he masturbated. All of it was reported in the press. Hickman listened to the words of friends, family, doctors, and law officials. The jury saw through his ruse – he was sane, and they knew it. So did he. Hickman had earlier stated that he would "swing" and still exhibited the same kind of detachment after the verdict was read.

While the prosecutors celebrated the verdict, Hickman's defense team was shocked. They could not fathom how Hickman, with his family history and the horrible crime he committed, had been determined to be sane, to be in full charge of his mental faculties.

Still fooled by his act, they began putting together a possible appeal.

On February 11, 1928, Hickman was back in court for sentencing by Judge Trabucco. Before that could happen, Jerome Walsh submitted a motion. He and Cantillon had been hard at work in a rather desperate attempt to save their client from the hangman's noose. They appeared in court with a four-page list of 20 specifically detailed reasons, arguing for Hickman's sentence to be deferred. Walsh's aim was to get Hickman a new trial, which would get them more time to bolster the insanity defense.

The motion challenged Judge Trabucco's presentation, the opinion of the jurors, defense objections that he felt were unfairly decided, that some of the testimonies read in court violated Hickman's Fifth Amendment rights, and more. Walsh also claimed that the defense had new evidence that had been gathered since the court adjourned after the jury's verdict.

Judge Trabucco stated that he would consider the defense motion and court was adjourned until Tuesday morning, February 14. When court reconvened that morning, Walsh had three more motions to submit: a motion in arrest of judgment, a formal motion for a new trial, and a nine-point list of objects that took issue with the court's jurisdiction. He was throwing everything at the wall, hoping that something would stick.

Needless to say, the prosecution objected to all of the motions, but during the hearing that followed, District Attorney Keyes re-called two witnesses: Dr. A.F. Wagner and Chief Herman Cline.

Dr. Wagner once again described the condition of Marion Parker's body during his examinations on December 17 and 18 and presented the gruesome morgue photographs that had been shown during the trial. He again indicated that he was a neighbor of the Parker family and that working on Marion's body had been the most difficult postmortem examination of his entire career.

Chief Herman Cline was visibly irritated at having to return to court and describe Hickman's crimes after he had already been found sane by a jury and judged to be aware of his acts. He was impatient with the process and offered only a truncated account of the manhunt. He offered highlights, noted a few of the details, and then added in some excerpts from Hickman's confession.

District Attorney Asa Keyes, who had to continue calling witnesses against Hickman, even after the jury's verdict had been handed down.

Walsh appeared flustered when he tried to have the testimonies of both men stricken from the record. The motion was denied – as well as all of the other motions that Walsh had come to court with on February 11, and on February 14.

The judge addressed the court, fully prepared with his sentence: "The court now determines and finds that the degree of crime in count two of the indictment is murder of the first degree without extenuating or mitigating circumstances."

Walsh and Cantillon sat back in their chairs, defeated.

Judge Trabucco continued, "William Edward Hickman, stand up."

Hickman rose from his chair and faced the judge. Looking directly into Judge Trabucco's eyes, he stood completely still. His eyes never wavered and his face showed no expression. This did not go unnoticed by the reporters in the courtroom.

The judge spoke again: "It is the judgment and sentence of his court, that for the crime of kidnapping, the offense described in count one of the indictment, that you, William Edward Hickman, be confined in the state prison of the state of California, at San Quentin, for the term prescribed by law, which term will be fixed by the Board of Prison directors."

The judge's eyes narrowed as he read the next part of the sentence, detailing the second count of the indictment against Hickman --- murder in the first degree. For that, he said, "you shall suffer the penalty of death."

Hickman was to be delivered by the Los Angeles County Sheriff to the warden at San Quentin, where he would be executed and put to death on Friday, April 27, 1928.

"And may God have mercy on your soul," the judge concluded.

Walsh and Cantillon were crushed. All their efforts had been for nothing, but they were not finished. They would do anything they could to try and reverse the sentence, or at worst, drag out the date of the execution as long as possible. Walsh, in fact, started immediately by moving that the death sentence be reversed on the grounds that Judge Trabucco was outside his jurisdiction as a visiting judge. That motion was also denied.

But they were not giving up. They were not working for their client merely as part of the legal process – they truly believed that Hickman was insane. Only a true madman, they believed, could kill and murder a little girl and then later claim that he loved her. They continued to repeat that insanity was proven by his family history. The jury had passed down its verdict, the judge had given out his sentence, but Walsh and Cantillon were not prepared to stop.

Although convicted and sentenced in the Parker case, Hickman's time in court was not yet over. He still had to go through the Ivy Thoms murder trial. This time, though, he was not alone – he was on trial with his old friend and crime partner, Welby Hunt. Hunt continued to deny that he had fired a gun during the robbery, even though ballistic tests proved that Thoms had been killed by a .38 – the gun that Hunt admitted carrying.

To the public, the Thoms trial was anticlimactic. It did not garner the headlines that the Parker case had. Hickman had already been sentenced to death and he could only die once. The fate of Welby Hunt was not interesting to the public. Hunt had never kidnapped and dismembered a child; he'd merely committed a robbery and allegedly shot a man while doing it. He was perceived as just another murderous punk who needed to be locked up. The trial lasted 16 days. At the end of it, both Hunt and

Hickman were found guilty of Thoms's murder. And Hickman, despite his best efforts, was once again declared to be sane.

Welby Hunt could not be hanged because he was a minor at the time of the murder, so he received a sentence of life in prison. He continued to claim that he was innocent of murder and expressed anger and hatred toward his former friend for turning him in. He swore that he had not fired the bullet that killed Ivy Thoms – Hickman did – and worse, Hickman knew it and allowed him to take the fall.

Hickman and Hunt were shackled together and taken to San Quentin on March 17, 1928. They did not speak during the trip.

Hickman was registered at San Quentin as inmate number 45041. During his medical examination, Hickman prattled on to his doctor about the murder and his impending execution. There is some speculation as to why Hickman decided to talk, with some believing that he was trying to achieve some prison notoriety for the murder.

Regardless of why he talked about the case, he blamed Perry Parker for making the mistake of trusting him. He said that Parker should have called the police the minute that he knew Marion had been kidnapped in spite of the note warning him not to do so. Hickman called himself a "master criminal." He told the doctor, "I felt no pity for the father. I felt no remorse at all. I just felt I was executing a master stroke. As for the little girl, she's better off than I am. At least she's out of this world of turmoil and strife. I no longer believe in heaven and hell, but I know she shall have everlasting life. Any man has the right to hold up another man if he wants to. Even if the holdup results in murder, it is all right. Everything is for-ordained. Our lives are mapped out for us from the beginning. What I have done is destiny. I could not help it."

While Hickman was settling into San Quentin's death row, his attorneys were still working to try and appeal his conviction. The verdict had generated a tangible public reaction. There were letters to newspapers across the country, most of them applauding the jury's decision. The public sent letters to the judge, the attorneys, and to officials at San Quentin. Some took it personally. There was more than one request that Hickman be hanged on a certain date, usually the letter writer's birthday.

Even in 1928, conspiracy theories were everywhere. Some insisted that Hickman had not acted alone, others claimed he was railroaded, that he was a "fall guy" for someone powerful, or that justice had not been served. Meetings were scheduled and grassroots efforts were made to get Hickman a new trial. Walsh and Cantillon had nothing to do with this movement, and law enforcement officials, along with the general public, generally ignored it. It received some marginal notoriety in the press, but faded quickly.

The appeals filed by Walsh and Cantillon did manage to extend Hickman's life. His execution date did not occur in April and Hickman lived on through the spring and summer in a cell on death row.

The press and the public were impatient. Letters from angry citizens filled the editorial pages of newspapers across the country. All of them wondered why it was taking so long "to put that monster away forever." The *Los Angeles Times* printed an editorial in August 1928 complaining about how the "Hickman situation" had dragged on for many months. It asked the question that so many others were asking: Why was Hickman still languishing on death row? The press and the public wanted to know, and the escalating reaction put pressure on law enforcement officials.

Perhaps as a result of public outcry, perhaps due to the newspaper editorials, or maybe because the defense had finally exhausted its efforts to save their client from the gallows, Warden James Holohan of San Quentin was ordered to execute Hickman on October 19, 1928.

Hickman spent the next few months preparing for his fate. As time ticked closer, Hickman sent off a flurry of letters to various police chiefs across the country, confessing to previously unknown crimes that he had committed – or that he said he'd committed. More likely, he was attempting to interest one of the police officials in one of the unknown cases, hoping that it might stall his execution. The ploy, if that's what it was, didn't work.

"I have made up my mind to take my medicine," Hickman wrote in a statement to the *Associated Press* from his cell at San Quentin. "I know very well that I have been a most guilty sinner. Nevertheless, I have confessed my sins and I am now trying to do what is right. I am sorry for having offended God and man. I desire punishment and ask no personal favors."

Hickman was making a show of religious convictions, but when he was not "confessing his sins", he was listening to jazz records on the phonograph in cell – sent to him by admirers – and writing replies to the many fan letters that he received each week. Apparently, people were as obsessed with brutal killers and depraved murderers in the 1920s as they are today.

When not entertaining his followers, Hickman was also writing letters to the families of his victims. He claimed that he was doing a spiritual cleansing to make amends for what he considered his past mistakes and remove these crimes from his damaged soul. He told the press that he was trying to "get right with God."

One of the letters that he wrote was to the widow of slain druggist Ivy Thoms. The letter was filled with religious platitudes and requests for her to not feel bitter toward her husband's killer. He signed the letter as "William Edward Hickman, the killer of Marion Parker," as if this was some sort of official title. It certainly was his claim to fame. The murder had given him status and notoriety, an infamy that his skills as a high school orator could have never offered.

The one letter that Hickman failed to write – the apology that he failed to offer – was to the Parker family. He never expressed his regret for his greatest crime. He continued to exploit it, though. He even admitted to reporters that he never should have attempted an insanity defense. He should have "stood up like a man and made my peace with God."

Of course, this didn't help Walsh's and Cantillon's efforts to keep Hickman off the gallows. By now, it seemed the killer was truly resigned to his fate.

Hickman only received a handful of visitors as the date of his execution drew closer. One of them was Welby Hunt, who had been sentenced to spend the rest of his life in prison. Hunt pleaded with Hickman to do something for him now that Hickman was about to hang. Hickman refused. Hickman said that he knew that Hunt had killed Ivy Thoms, no matter what he was telling others. Hickman said that he would only help his former friend if he could do so without lying. Hunt should embrace God, Hickman said. As he walked away from Hickman's cell, Hunt's face was flushed with anger.

Welby Hunt did serve a long prison term, but he was eventually released. After serving many years with a record of good behavior, he was paroled and settled in California. He died in Rancho Mirage on May 26, 1995, at the age of 84. During those rare times when he spoke about his past, he maintained that he was innocent of the crime that had kept him behind bars for most of his life. He always insisted that Hickman had pulled the trigger.

Perhaps Hickman's most surprising prison visitor was his father. William Hickman, Sr. had deserted him as a child, initially disowned him after he was arrested for murder, but had a change of heart and testified on his behalf at trial. He came to San Quentin to tell his son goodbye. He obtained permission for a private visit and stayed for nearly an hour. Reporters were waiting for Mr. Hickman when he left the prison. His face was pale and he had been crying. "The boy is very brave," he told the newsmen. "I thought I'd console him, but he consoled me instead. He said he loved the Parker girl and was sorry he killed her. He told me to live a Christian life and he'd see me in a little while. He gave me a message for his mother. I will give it to her and nobody else."

Eva Hickman never visited her son before his execution. There were rumors that she was on her way to the prison at the last minute – Warden Holohan even allowed extra time before the execution – but the stories weren't true. She never saw her son again. Perhaps the message delivered by her former husband was enough.

Hickman wrote more letters, including one to Chief Tom Gurdane of Pendleton, Oregon, the man who had captured him. He apologized to Gurdane for pretending to be insane when he was incarcerated there. He would also apologize to Warden Holohan before his execution for all the trouble that he'd caused. The warden had been barraged with calls and letters from unstable women, pleading with him to save Hickman's life.

Hickman spent the majority of his time with Father William Fleming, the prison chaplain, who spent as much time as possible with condemned prisoners. He spent long hours listening to Hickman's feelings about God, about salvation, and about forgiveness. He told the priest, "I'm not afraid anymore. I'm not afraid to die. I sent letters to everyone I could, asking for forgiveness and understanding. I spent many nights praying to God that He forgive me. I believe we will all meet in the hereafter."

Before leaving Hickman for the last time, Father Fleming gave him Holy Communion and Hickman told him that he took great peace in the priest's visit.

To the very end, Hickman couldn't help but try to fool people. He had an engrained need to show how superior he was to everyone by making them believe whatever he wanted them to believe. That's the opinion of this author – but why do I think so?

I find it very telling that the one letter of apology that Hickman never wrote was to the Parker family. I am convinced that they would have seen through his lies. Hickman was not sorry for anything that he had done. All his talk of God and salvation at the end was nothing more than an extension of his phony insanity plea. Sadly, many of the people to whom he apologized actually took him at his word, and believed he felt remorse, just as his hard-working attorneys believed that he really was insane. William Hickman wasn't crazy – he was a devious sociopath who knew exactly what he was doing all along.

Visits by priests, religious messages to his father and mother, letters of apology – all these things were a sham, just like the bogus insanity claim. Hickman proved it himself, on the very night before his execution, when he finally offered his most chilling confession of all to prison guard Charles Alston.

William Edward Hickman was an evil man.

On the night of October 18, Hickman couldn't sleep. Restless and looking for conversation, he called out to Alston and told him that he wanted to talk. Bored, Alston walked over to face the notorious killer of Marion Parker. The guard was a family man, with children of his own. Two of them were close to Marion's age when she died. He despised Hickman and later admitted that it was hard to resist the urge to spit in the cocky young man's face. Even so, he had questions that he wanted to ask, and he did.

"Why did you kill Marion Parker?" he asked.

Alston expected the usual answer. He'd read everything that Hickman had said to reporters and he expected Hickman to tell him the same thing. He didn't, though. Hickman just shrugged. "Because I got tired of finding her in the room where I kept her while I was trying to get the ransom money. It got so the sight of her face drove me into a frenzy."

Alston didn't believe him at first. That was the reason? Hickman murdered the girl simply because he was sick of looking at her? After nearly a year's worth of headlines, a sensational trial, a series of confessions that became stranger and more gruesome as time went on, Hickman finally stated that he killed Marion because she was an inconvenience. His "great crime" of kidnapping for ransom had worked smoothly until the botched Friday night exchange and after Marion became irritating about it, he killed her. There was no mention of Providence, no visions that told him to do it – nothing. Hickman just felt like it because she annoyed him.

"Why didn't you just drop her off in front of her house and leave the state?" Alston asked.

Hickman shrugged a little. "It's funny you should say that. Marion said the same thing. I almost did it, but I thought she would scream and alert the police guards at the Parker home before I could make a clean getaway." Hickman shook his head and sat down on his bunk. He looked up at the guard and added, "That's where I used bad judgment."

Alston started to walk away, disgusted with the conversation and disgusted with Hickman himself.

But Hickman kept on talking. "I used bad judgment all the way through. I could have robbed a bank, got 10 times more, and would have suffered far less serious consequences when captured." He sighed and continued, "I guess it was the most terrible crime in the history of the world. If ever a mortal deserved to be hanged, I do."

Hickman just couldn't help himself. He had to just keep bragging, still needing attention even as he waited to die. He still wasn't finished talking and Alston was not finished listening.

He admitted to the prison guard what he'd been lying to his lawyers about for months. "I wasn't crazy when I killed the Parker girl. I would have killed my best friend to get what I wanted."

Alston was now ready to walk away. It was the general consensus among law enforcement officers that Hickman had been lying all along. They'd heard the stories of the show that he put on in Oregon and his antics at the county jail. Alston was not surprised to hear the killer admit it.

But Hickman still wasn't finished. He looked up at Alston with a smirk – the same confident smirk that Mary Holt had seen that day at Marion Parker's school. It was the one that exuded such confidence and convinced Mrs. Holt to allow Marion to leave the school with the man who killed her two days later. Alston didn't like Hickman's smirk, or his smug behavior.

Hickman continued smiling at the guard and then looked directly into Alston's eyes. He spoke, "I got a kick out of dissecting Marion's corpse."

Alston was stunned with rage. A lesser man might have opened the cell door and beaten Hickman into silence. A worse man might have killed him on the spot. But Alston silently turned away, his teeth and fists tightly clenched. And as he walked away down the corridor, he could hear Hickman laughing behind him.

As the clock ticked closer to the execution, Jerome Walsh was still pleading Hickman's case. On October 10, he had petitioned Governor C.C. Young for commutation of the death sentence. The governor issued a statement: "I will treat the Hickman case as any other that might come before me. I will not grant executive clemency unless there is some new and positive evidence proving the innocence of the prisoner."

Of course, no such evidence existed.

But Walsh didn't stop working. He went to the state capitol in Sacramento and met with Governor Young on October 15. The governor pointed out that the state constitution provided that a twice-convicted felon could not seek commutation of sentence without assent of a majority of the members of the state supreme court. Not surprisingly, that assent was not forthcoming.

Walsh fought until the very end, but there was nothing he could do to save his client. Hickman was right – he was going to "swing."

Just as the murder, manhunt, capture, and trial had filled the nation's newspapers, every detail leading up to Hickman's execution was widely reported. Aside from the rumors that Eva Hickman was going to be present to see her son die – in the end, she did not – the most persistent claim was that Perry Parker and his son planned to be present at the execution. Parker remained silent about this for several weeks, trying to ignore the press accounts, and to protect his family from further pain. He was tired of all the hoopla surrounding his daughter's murderer and wanted to allow his family to heal emotionally after such a tragedy. Parker had believed that once the trial and sentencing were over, the press would finally leave them alone. But that was not the case.

The press remained persistent, and soon the rumors were running so rampant that his friends and coworkers expected him to take the trip to San Quentin. Parker tried to ignore the stories until finally he could be silent no more. He reluctantly called a press conference and made an official statement.

He told the assembled reporters: "Certainly, I'll not attend. Such reports are absurd. That is furthest removed from my mind. The execution means nothing to us except that the law is taking its course. We have no desire to be present; none whatsoever. In the execution we recognize only one more link in that inevitable chain of events that must be wielded before we can forget. Since the trial we have had only one desire: to have it all over with, so that we can begin healing from our wounds and forgetting our loss. Removal of this man is necessary to that end. When he is gone, when he is dead, there will be that much less left to bring back to us the memory of what we have lost and what we have suffered."

Perry Parker just wanted his family to be left alone. He wanted to return to the peaceful anonymity that his family had once enjoyed. Their lives had been peaceful and pleasant. They were a happy family that had been viciously struck by terrible tragedy. Parker was tired – tired of the police, the press, the trial, and the well-meaning public. He was worn down by strangers recognizing him on the street and offering consoling words. He knew they meant well, and he appreciated their concern, but words could not bring back his beloved child.

Marion would never be able to return home.

Parker just wanted to put his arms around the rest of his family and bring them some peace from the horror of Marion's murder. He wasn't asking for much – just a return to the life they had enjoyed before that terrible day in December.

The Parkers tried to separate themselves from the tragedy, but they were not quite ready to let it go, even almost a year later. A train set that Marion had played with on the day before her disappearance was still set up on the floor of the Parker's living room. And each afternoon, at the time that Marion had normally arrived home from school, her dog still looked out the front window and cried.

On October 18 – the evening before he showed his true face to guard Charles Alston -- Hickman was removed from his cell and mounted the 75 steps from the inner yard to the old shops building that housed the death cell, which opened only to the scaffold. As taps sounded at 9:00 p.m., Warden Holohan went to the cell that was occupied by Hickman and another murderer, Russell St. Clair Beitzel, and rapped on the door. Hickman immediately stepped forward, bidding his cellmate goodbye, and was taken out to the steel runway that flanked the cell house as a balcony.

The death cell was composed of two wooden-barred cages, fitted only with a mattress and two blankets, which was in the center of a room that was 13-feet square on the third floor of the old shops building. The room was double-lined with steel mesh.

After entering the cell, Hickman knelt down and began to pray. As he prayed, he looked at the signs, symbols and markings that his predecessors had left on the walls as their last words to the world. To Hickman's right was the door that opened to the gallows.

On the morning of Friday, October 19 – execution day – Warden James Holohan and Father William Fleming arrived at Hickman's cell door.

It was 9:50 a.m. and the hangman was waiting.

Hickman had been given a breakfast of eggs, prunes, a roll, and some coffee. He had picked at it and drank a little of the coffee. He stood, dressed in a new black suit, as Warden Holohan entered his cell and read the formal order of execution. Hickman listened impatiently and then cried out, "Now, let me read you something!" Hands shaking, he read aloud the last letter that he had received from his mother, then burst into tears.

It was time to go. Hickman shuffled from the cell. His ankles were chained and his arms were now tied to his sides. Two large, burly guards walked on either side of him. His confidence and his smugness were gone. He was now just another murderer whose life was going to end.

The cluster of men traveled to the gallows room. There were a dozen witnesses, most of them journalists covering the event. As Hickman got closer, the voices got louder. The group slowly approached the platform. Hickman looked pale and nervous and sweat had appeared on his brow.

Hickman did not climb the 13 scaffold steps with the "unfaltering treads" that he had predicted he would. His foot was noticeably shaking as he lifted it onto the first step. About halfway up the steps, he slumped over and the guards, with a hand under each arm, had to help him. As they did so, his old bravado returned for a moment. He flung his head back and turned his face towards the whitewashed ceiling of the death chamber and began to pray. His lips moved and his face twitched. No one around him could hear or understand the words.

Hickman was asked if he had anything to say.

He shook his head. Finally, the killer was done talking.

He never asked for mercy as the black hood was dropped over his head, but then, the man who murdered a young girl just for the thrill of it, fainted.

His body sagged and fell sideways. He was unconscious. In that second, the hangman raised his hand and three men poised with knives behind a screen on the gallows platform simultaneously drew their blades across three strings. One of the strings released the trap door and Hickman's slumped form slipped through. But, thanks to the faint, his neck did not break. He wasn't instantly killed, as was the standard method of execution. Because he had fainted in the way he had, his weight had shifted and when he fell, the noose strangled him to death.

It was just the way he had strangled Marion Parker.

Hickman's body dangled at the end of the rope, flailing and jerking about as the rope choked the life from him. He gurgled and coughed as he twisted back and forth.

There was a noise below. One of the spectators had fainted. His wooden chair toppled over as he fell. Some of the reporters watched, some looked away, and the rest scribbled furiously on their notepads. Another spectator fainted at the sight of the body flailing on the rope. His chair crashed to the floor. And then a reporter joined him. His pen skittered across the floor as it fell from his fingers.

The prison physician, Dr. Ralph Becker, edged closely to the dangling body. He put a stethoscope to Hickman's chest and listened for a heartbeat. It was still there. He shook his head and waited for the last death throes of the body to occur. He tried again and this time, there was nothing. It took William Edward Hickman almost 15 minutes to die.

The *Los Angeles Times* noted, "Hickman is dead and the world is cleaner for his going. His page is turned and the rest of the pages are brighter by contrast. The Hickman case is over. Now let's forget it."

But no one was ready to forget it, not just yet – especially the lingering spirit of a little girl who met her cruel demise many years before her time.

HAUNTED

In the final days of 1927 and throughout most of 1928, the Marion Parker case was one of the most sensational, heartbreaking stories in America. People from all over the country eagerly read about every detail of the murder in the newspapers, watched the newsreels in their local cinemas, and heard it discussed on the radio. The story found its way into the roots music and folk songs of the time. Murder ballads were an especially popular form of entertainment, keeping the memories of the slain alive for years after they were gone. Those kinds of songs – made popular by singers like Woody Guthrie and Hughie "Leadbelly" Ledbetter – reflected the times, the culture, and the news.

There was an African-American spiritual called "California Kidnapping" by Reverend J.M. Gates that compared the case to his own family's past. He stated that, like this California kidnapping, his "grandmother and grandfather were kidnapped out of the deepest darkest jungles of Africa. Bloodhounds chased them. Then Abraham Lincoln with the stroke of a pen, freed poor Negroes and half Negro men." It wasn't exactly the same thing, but the sentiment was there.

There were other songs, too. There was "The Fate of Edward Hickman" by Blind Andy, released just after Hickman was sentenced to die, and "The Marion Parker Murder" by John McGhee, which came out in March 1928. There was the prophetic "The Hanging of the Fox" by Vernon Dalhart, using the name Al Craven, which came out on April 5, 1928, a good six months before Hickman went to the gallows. Another 1928 song called "Little Marion Parker," included the lyrics:

Way out in California, a family bright and gay
Were planning for a Christmas not so very far away;
They had a little daughter, a sweet and pretty child,
And all the folks that knew her loved Marion Parker's smile.

She left her home one morning for a school not far away,
And no one dreamed that danger was lurking near that day.
But then a murderous villain, a friend with heart of stone,
Took little Marion Parker away from friends and home.

The world was horror-stricken, the people held their breath
Until they found poor Marion, her body cold in death.
They hunted for the coward, young Hickman was their man;
They brought him back to justice, his final trial to stand.

The jury found him guilty, Of course they could not fail;
He must be executed, soon in San Quentin Jail.
And while he waits his sentence, let's hope he learns to pray,
To make his black soul ready for the great Judgment Day.

There is a great commandment, that says 'Thou Shall not Kill!'
And those who do not heed it, their cup of sorrow fill.
This song should be a warning to parents near and far,
We cannot guard too closely, the ones we love so dear.

Interestingly, the song was sung to the tune of another murder ballad called "Mary Phagan," a 1913 sex crime that occurred in Georgia and had political repercussions in the region. As varied as the stories and the lyrics were, the songs were performed with the same basic tune.

Of course, such songs didn't get a lot of airplay outside of rural radio stations. They were pressed into records, but with a limited audience, they faded away over time.

Unfortunately, so did the Marion Parker story.

William Edward Hickman, found guilty and executed for one of the most grisly child abductions in American history, believed that he would become as famous as Leopold and Loeb – a reasonable expectation, given the widespread shock and horror provoked by the crime. But apart from mostly hard-core true crime buffs, few remember his name today. Leopold and Loeb, however, the Jazz Age "thrill killers" continue to be the subjects of books, plays, and even films.

Why? Well, it seems the story of Hickman and Marion Parker reveals an interesting point about American society. While inordinately gruesome or macabre crimes might appeal to a primal human need for morbid excitement, they are not necessarily the ones that exert the deepest fascination on the public. The crimes that come to define an era tend to be those that reflect its most pressing anxieties. To most people in the 1920s, for example, the pampered, elitist, college-age hedonists Leopold and Loeb were the living embodiments of the out-of-control "Flaming Youth" of the period – just as, four decades later, Charles Manson and his depraved followers seemed like every parent's worst nightmares about sex- and drug-crazed hippies.

In Marion Parker's time, parents were not yet fearing for the safety of their children as they would later. Yes, they warned them not to talk to strangers, but thought nothing of letting them stay out after dark, play freely throughout the neighborhood, ride a streetcar to school, or even travel alone to go shopping or see a movie. Children were not often kidnapped – aside from a few isolated cases – and the story did not manage to define the fears of the era. And it faded away.

But Marion was not forgotten by those who knew her. In fact, it's not out of line to say that everyone involved in the case was "haunted" by her in some way.

Once Hickman was dead, Perry Parker told the press that he was glad that it was over and that he intended on continuing to help his family get back to normal. It was something that he had been trying to do since the trial. They would move past this horrible time in their lives for good. Marion would remain in his heart, he said, but he no longer wanted to be haunted by the lifeless, dismembered body that he had held in his arms. Of course, he never really got past it.

After the final Hickman articles vanished from the papers, the Parkers eventually became yesterday's news. New stories, crimes, and sensations came along and Perry Parker was finally left alone. He never spoke to the press again.

Parker lived 16 more years, still mourning the daughter that he had lost. His passing in 1944, at the age of only 57, was barely noticed by the press.

Geraldine Parker lived until 1963, when she died of cancer at age 75. Although decades had passed since Marion's death, the local press did carry a story about her passing. The headline read, "Mother of Kidnap Case Figure Dies," and it offered some cursory background about Marion's murder.

Geraldine had moved to San Diego three years after Perry Parker's death, and at the time she died, she was living with her daughter, Marjorie Parker Holmes, and Marjorie's husband. Marjorie had achieved her own level of infamy in the late 1920s simply due to being the twin who was spared by the killer. Marjorie had been shielded from the media by her father and there is no record of her ever publicly discussing Marion's kidnapping or murder later in life. Marjorie was still living in San Diego when she passed away on August 2, 1987, at the age of 71.

Perry Parker, Marion and Marjorie's older brother, went on to become the chief of plant protection and safety for the Northrop Corporation in Hawthorne, California. He had a daughter and two grandchildren – and never forgot his lost little sister. He passed away in Los Angeles on April 8, 1983, just three months before his 76th birthday.

Jerome K. Walsh, Hickman's first attorney, had a long and distinguished legal career. He was a friend of Harry S. Truman – many of his papers can be found today in the Truman Presidential Library – and played a large role in bringing down organized crime figures in Kansas City. He wed Mary Lawler in the summer of 1928 and his son, Jerome, Jr., followed in his father's footsteps and became one of the lead investigators of the My Lai Massacre during the Vietnam War.

Richard Cantillon died in 1967. Just before his death, he wrote a book about the Hickman case, but it did not go into print until five years later. The book, *In Defense of the Fox*, was published posthumously in 1972 by a small press and is long out of print. It is one of the few books ever written by an attorney who failed to prove his client's innocence. Despite everything, Cantillon went to his grave still believing that Hickman was insane. It reads as though Cantillon blamed himself for Hickman's execution, much in the same way that Mary Holt blamed herself for allowing Marion to be taken from school that afternoon. It is said that Mrs. Holt eventually died in a mental institution. Cantillon's guilt never went to that extreme.

Asa Keyes, the Los Angeles District Attorney who played the lead role in Hickman's prosecution, achieved a loft level of celebrity status during the 1920s. He had been involved in the 1926 "kidnapping" case that involved evangelist Sister Aimee Semple McPherson and, of course, in the Marion Parker case. But the district attorney's glory days did not last for long. In 1929, a little more than a year after the Hickman trial, Keyes was on trial himself and was he was found guilty of accepting a bribe from the Julian Petroleum Company. Keyes was sentenced to five years imprisonment, but was pardoned by Governor James Rolph in August 1933. After his release, Keyes waged an unsuccessful fight to win reinstatement of his law license, but the bar association opposed him. He died at the age of only 57 in October 1934. Friends said that his years in San Quentin had destroyed his health.

The story of Marion Parker was overshadowed by not only the murder of Bobby Franks at the hands of Leopold and Loeb, but also by the 1932 kidnapping and murder of famous aviator Charles Lindbergh's infant son. Lindbergh had been at the height of his fame in 1927 when Marion Parker was kidnapped and killed. During the press reports of the Lindbergh kidnapping, the Parker case was referred to often, but the two more famous cases eventually washed away the story of Marion's cruel death.

Even the ghost story attached to the Leopold and Loeb case is more famous.

After their convictions, Leopold and Loeb were sent to Joliet Penitentiary. Loeb was murdered there. After his death, his attorney, Clarence Darrow once stated, "He is better off dead. For him, death is an easier sentence.

Leopold, who like his accomplice had received a sentence of life in prison, plus 99 years for kidnapping, remained locked away for decades. Finally, in 1958, poet Carl Sandburg successfully pleaded his fourth appeal. Leopold was released, moved to Puerto Rico, got married, and devoted the rest of his life to helping the poor. He died of heart failure in August 1971, bringing an end to the harrowing story.

There were stories that claimed that sending Leopold and Loeb to prison for the murder of young Bobby Franks did not bring an end to the tragic case. There was a story of a ghost who took nearly 50 years to find peace.

During those years, visitors to Rosehill Cemetery on the north side of Chicago often reported the apparition of a young boy standing among the stones and mausoleums in the Jewish section of the graveyard. It was there where the Franks family mausoleum was located, although its location was not listed on any maps of the cemetery and employees were long instructed not to point it out to curiosity-seekers. Even so, this tomb could be discovered within the confines of the beautiful burial ground and starting in the 1920s, maintenance workers and visitors alike encountered the ghostly boy. Many came to believe that it was the ghost of Bobby Franks, unable to rest in the wake of his bloody and violent death.

The boy was often seen wandering the grounds, but only from a distance. Whenever he was approached, the apparition would vanish. These sightings continued for years, but eventually, they came to an end – in 1971. I don't believe that it's a coincidence that this was at the exact same time that Nathan Leopold died in Puerto Rico.

With the last of his murderers gone, perhaps Bobby Franks was finally able to find peace on the other side.

But what about Marion Parker?

In the middle 1980s, one of the classic books on Los Angeles crime, *Fallen Angels: Chronicles of LA Crime and Mystery*, was published by authors Marvin J. Wolf and Katherine Mader. One of the stories featured in the book is a short account of the brutal murder of Marion Parker. In this case, though, the crime story came with a chilling supernatural twist.

According to the authors, most of the book was put together with Wolf doing the writing and Mader doing the research. When it came to the Parker story, though, Wolf had a good friend who lived in the neighborhood where the kidnapping occurred and he called her to get an address for another case. Wolf remarked that the friend happened to live very close to the former Parker residence and the friend said that she was casually acquainted with the current owners of the house. They had only purchased it the year before. Perhaps, she suggested, they might have some relevant information or old photos.

Wolf telephoned one of the owners of the Parker house, a 33-year-old graduate student named Michelle Pelland. She had never heard of Marion Parker and did not know anything about the connection of the house on South Wilton Place to one of L.A.'s infamous crimes. She listened with interest as Wolf told her about the kidnapping and murder.

As he spoke, though, she suddenly interrupted him, "Oh, that accounts for our ghost."

"Ghost?" Wolf asked.

Pelland explained, "Yes, I call it a ghost, but it's not at all frightening." She said that one of the main reasons that she, graduate student Steve Daley, and accountant Ed Harris pooled their resources and bought the house in the first place was because they got such a good feeling from it. She said, "It felt like there had been a lot of love in the house."

About nine months after they moved in, though, Daley began to notice something strange. Steve Daley later spoke with Wolf. He explained, "I'm a skeptic. I'm very reluctant to say that it's some kind of physical manifestation of a spirit, but there is definitely something here. I've always had the feeling in this house that we've been sharing the space with something. But it's not intrusive. I first noticed it after we got a kitten. Many cats are prowlers. They're all over the house. But not mine. This is a lap cat. Always stays very close. I'm often home alone, working on a school paper, or catnapping, or just quietly reading. And I hear footsteps. Sometimes I hear somebody on the stairs. At first I thought it was the cat, but it was always right next to me in plain sight. Then I started to listen more carefully. It's not just the sounds of an old house settling. There's definitely another presence in the house. But I never notice it when there's anybody else home."

Daley spoke of other encounters with the eerie "something" in the house, stating that there seemed to be a softness to the presence, which led him to believe that it was a small child. He continued, "One afternoon as I went down the stairs I felt – I saw something out of the corner of my eye. I turned my head and there was nothing. Maybe it was only a flash of light from the street – but I know I *felt* something get out of my way. Until I learned about the kidnapping, the spirit, or whatever it is, didn't have a name. Now I'm inclined to call it Marion."

The ghost manifested itself in various ways. The owners of the house once had an Irish Setter named Max, a skittish dog that bolted at sudden noises – and often at things that no one else heard. One day, he reacted so strangely to some unknown noise or movement, ran out of the front door that had been mysteriously opened, and never returned.

There were also objects that inexplicably moved about in the kitchen. Daley told Wolf, "Sometimes things get moved from the center of the table, but I'm the only one in the house. I'm sort of absent-minded, sometimes, but there have been several times when I'm very sure I put a dish or a cup in a certain place. I've been home all alone, but it's been moved somewhere else when I see it next."

Michelle Pelland told Wolf that she often felt something when she entered an upstairs bedroom that had always unexplainably referred to as "the kid's bedroom." "It's a benevolent spirit," she was convinced. "It knows when somebody is afraid. Then it stays out. My son, Nathan, hears it a lot. He's had the feeling that something was there. But it wasn't a threatening presence." When he first began to notice the presence of the spirit, Nathan was 12 – the same age as Marion Parker when she was kidnapped.

When Pelland and Wolf first spoke about the house, it was a dark and unusually stormy night in mid-December. Purely by chance, it also happened to be the anniversary of the week when Marion Parker was kidnapped and murdered in 1927. When Wolf described Marion's eventual fate, an eerie thing occurred. "I thought you'd like to know that all of the lights in this house are going on and off," Pelland gasped into the telephone. Daley, who was sitting nearby, confirmed it.

Pelland shuddered, "My hair is standing on end."

He wasn't afraid to admit it later – so was Marvin Wolf's.

Since that time, and as recently as the late 1990s, others who have lived in the house have also reported eerie events. One family said that they often heard weird noises, some of which sounded like a child calling out. According to some stories, a séance was later conducted in the house and psychics confirmed that the resident spirit really was that of Marion Parker, still occupying the house where she had once lived happily with her family.

After Marion was taken by the "Fox," the only thing she wanted was to be back home with her sister, brother, and her parents. This was a little girl who didn't like to be away from home after dark. When the ransom exchange was botched on Friday night, she begged her abductor to just take her home, drop her off in her driveway, and drive away. She would have done anything to go home again. That was all she wanted – to go home.

It looks like after all of these years, she's finally made it.

BIBLIOGRAPHY

Alix, Ernest – *Ransom Kidnapping in America;* 1978
Allen, Frederick Lewis – *Only Yesterday;* 1931
Blanche, Tony & Brad Schreiber – *Death in Paradise;* 1998
Burt, Olive Wooley – *American Murder Ballads;* 1958
Cantillon, Richard – *In Defense of the Fox;* 1972
Caughey, John & Laree Caugey – *Los Angeles: Biography of a City;* 1976
Dunn, Katherine – *Death Scenes;* 1996
Epstein, Daniel Mark - *Sister Aimee: The Life of Aimee Semple McPherson;* 1994
Fass, Paula S. – *Kidnapped: Child Abduction in America;* 1997
Heimann, Jim – *Sins of the City;* 1999
Newton, Michael – *Stolen Away;* 2000
Neibaur, James L. – *Butterfly in the Rain;* 2016
Schechter, Harold – *Deranged;* 1990
--------------------- ---*Psycho USA;* 2012
Sifakis, Carl – *Encyclopedia of American Crime;* 1982
Smith, James R. & W. Lane Rogers – *The California Snatch Racket;* 2010
Stanley, Leo G. – *Men at their Worst;* 1940
Taylor, Troy – *Bloody Hollywood;* 2008
-------------- - *Murder & Mayhem on Chicago's South Side;* 2010
Wolf, Marvin J. & Katherine Nader – *Fallen Angels;* 1986
Wride, Tim B. (Essay / Introduction by James Ellroy) *Scene of the Crime;* 2004

Newspapers
Chicago Daily Tribune
Kansas City Star
Los Angeles Daily News
Los Angeles Examiner
Los Angeles Herald
Los Angeles Times
New York Times

Special Thanks to:
April Slaughter: Cover Design and Artwork
Lois Taylor: Editing and Proofreading
Lisa Taylor Horton and Lux
Haven and Helayna Taylor
Orrin Taylor
Rene Kruse
Rachael Horath
Elyse and Thomas Reihner
Bethany Horath
Mary DeLong
Ken Melvoin-Berg
John Winterbauer
The entire crew of American Hauntings and American Hauntings Ink

And to all the readers who have been kind enough to buy my books and maintain an interest in my strange little world for – at the time of this publication – 23 years now. I know that I don't always make it easy to like all the books that I write, but thanks for helping me to continue to do what I love.

ABOUT THE AUTHOR

Troy Taylor is the author of more than 120 books on ghosts, hauntings, true crime, the unexplained, and the supernatural in America. He is also the founder of American Hauntings Ink, which offers books, ghost tours, events, and weekend excursions. He was born and raised in the Midwest and currently divides his time between Illinois and the far-flung reaches of America.